GOD'S FINGERPRINTS

Journey Into The Hands Of God

ROMI VERDERA

Published by
Breath Of The Spirit Foundation, Inc.
20 Thornycroft Ave.,
Staten Island, NY 10312

ISBN:978-0-578-24480-8
Printed in the USA

Phone: 1-347-301-2833
E-mail: verdera2006@yahoo.com
www.RomiVerdera.tv

This book is dedicated to
my wife Rosavilla,
my sons Jeremy and Jason,
and their wives Eulix and Nellie,
and my five grandchildren,
Angel, Juliana,
Jaylene, Celestia
and Christian.

CONTENTS

PREFACE

Slow Down and Read Meditatively

There is an English adage that says, "A picture is worth a thousand words." In this book, when you see a picture with a Scripture, it is meant to lead you into a meditation of those thousand words. I have personally meditated over and over these particular Scriptures for many years and they have become a part of my awareness and worldview. So, I urge you not to hurriedly read the pages of this book. God gave us eternity. You have plenty of time. You have all the time and your hurried pace is just caused by modern life's illusion that you have no time for reflective meditation of your life with God. If you would just jot down a sample of how every hour was used by you in a single day, you will discover how much time you waste every day on unimportant matter. The Scriptures quoted in this book are parts of the Bible that I have daily and repeatedly reflected on until they become real in my life. Do not let them become just passing thoughts in your mind that missed to fill the hunger of your heart. There is a process by which these truths become your own and that is by keeping the thought longer in your awareness repeatedly until they seep into your subconscious mind, into your heart and spirit and be a transforming power inside of you.

———

Memorize and Ponder

Peace I leave with you; My peace I give you. I do not give to you as the world gives. Do not let your hearts be troubled and do not be afraid. (John 14:27)

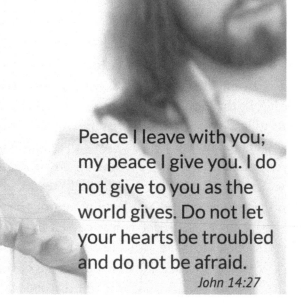

Peace I leave with you; my peace I give you. I do not give to you as the world gives. Do not let your hearts be troubled and do not be afraid.
John 14:27

You keep him in perfect peace whose mind is stayed on you, because he trusts in you. (Isaiah 26:3)

Peace Is a Gift From God

Peace of heart and mind is a gift from Jesus Christ. Like any other gift, it becomes ours if we know how to receive it, unpack it, keep it, and enjoy it. Jesus has done His part of giving. But if we do not know how to receive it and enjoy it, we will miss His gift of peace. The way to receive it and keep it is by meditation of His words, and abiding in His words. That is why this book is not for fast reading. I urge you to stop a lot as you read this book and ponder. Use the pictures to plunge you into meditation of God's words. I specifically inclined the letters and separated God's words into its own paragraph to highlight them to your attention. Reflect on them, contemplate on them, make them your own. Like food properly chewed and digested, which in turn nourishes the body, the words in this book are a bread of life that needs to be digested in the mind and heart and be a powerful truth in your spirit that will manifest in your life. Let the peace of God which surpasses understanding, be real inside of you. I pray that God opens your mind and heart, slows you down in your hurried pace of life, and grants you the peace you are seeking after. Amen.

You keep him in perfect peace whose mind is stayed on You, because he trusts in You.

Isaiah 26:3

Chapter One

INTRODUCTION

"Let anyone who is thirsty come to me and drink..." (John 7:37)

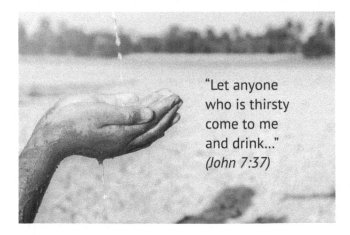

"Let anyone who is thirsty come to me and drink..." (John 7:37)

———

God Touched Me

This is not a book of dry knowledge. You are holding this book because you are thirsty. You are dissatisfied with just "knowing about" God and you want "to experience" God in your heart. There will be lots of time when you would want to lay down this book and taste the truth that is touching your soul. You want to continue drinking of the truth flowing into your soul. When that moment comes, stop reading. This is a book written to make you experience God's presence.

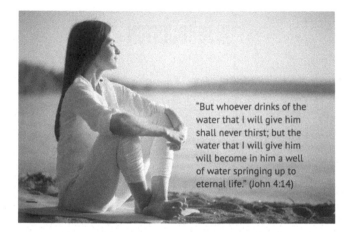

"But whoever drinks of the water that I will give him shall never thirst; but the water that I will give him will become in him a well of water springing up to eternal life." (John 4:14)

"But whoever drinks of the water that I will give him shall never thirst; but the water that I will give him will become in him a well of water springing up to eternal life." (John 4:14)

I heartily and prayerfully wrote this, and as I dwell in God's presence in meditation, God reminds me of the moments of His touch in my life as His fingerprints got impressed on me. His presence and power are extended in this book. It is intended to bring you to God's presence and make you experience Him, hear Him, see Him. Is that too much to ask of Him? No. His desire to be close to you is more than your craving to be intimate with Him. He has been waiting for you for so long for this moment. So you should be still and pray first before you continue to read and ask God to touch you.

God our Father gave us Jesus His son who revealed the love of the Father to us. Jesus breathe on us his Holy Spirit who unites us with the Father and the Son. You and I will be at the center of this dance of the Holy Trinity One God as you read this book.

And the Holy Spirit descended on him in bodily form like a dove. And a voice came from heaven: "You are my Son, whom I love; with you I am well pleased." (Luke 3:22 NIV)

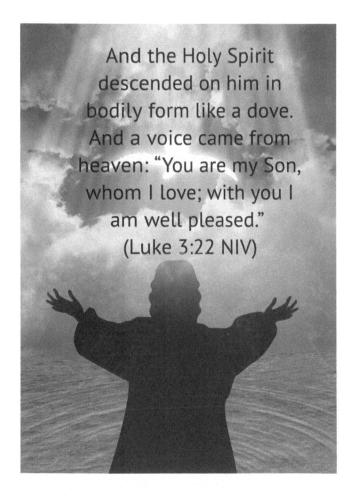

And the Holy Spirit descended on him in bodily form like a dove. And a voice came from heaven: "You are my Son, whom I love; with you I am well pleased." (Luke 3:22 NIV)

When you sense that you are having a glimpse of God's fingerprints on any part of your reading, I mean a sense of God's revelation of truth, a feeling of God's love, you should pause and ponder.

Meditate and pray as you sense God's touch on your mind and heart. Do not read hurriedly. There is no shortness of time in God's presence. God gave you all eternity. In this deep prayerful moments that you will experience as you read, heaven will come down on earth. You will long for this breakthrough and it will happen every now and then as a joyful taste of your face-to-face encounter with Him in glory in eternity. Do not rush! Ask God to let you into His presence and let you join in the dance of your life with God which He orchestrated for you. When He lets you, you would have experienced the reality of God whom you just "know about" before, but now, you are beginning to "know Him" as Jesus knows Him. This is Jesus' prayer:

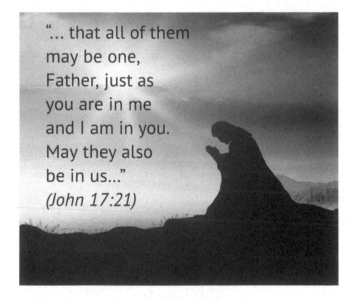

"... that all of them may be one, Father, just as you are in me and I am in you. May they also be in us..." (John 17:21)

"that all of them may be one, Father, just as you are in me and I am in you. May they also be in us..."(John 17:21)

———

Chapter Two

BOOK BORN IN A DREAM

"For God does speak—now one way, now another, —though no one perceives it. In a dream, in a vision of the night, when deep sleep falls on people as they slumber in their beds." (Job 33:14-15)

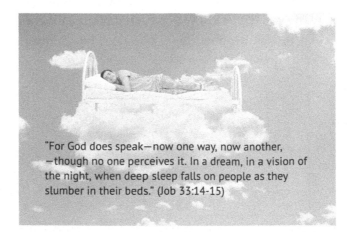

"For God does speak—now one way, now another, —though no one perceives it. In a dream, in a vision of the night, when deep sleep falls on people as they slumber in their beds." (Job 33:14-15)

God Touched Me

On the morning of my 65th birthday, I woke up with this crystal clear thought of writing a book and the title would be "GOD'S FINGERPRINTS." Was I dreaming? Or was it a simple mental impression? There was no sound of a voice coming from heaven. Was it just a simple thought that crossed my mind while I was half awake? All I know is that it is just a knowing. This is God's assignment. Throughout my life, every now and then, I had these very clear thoughts or impressions in my mind as soon as I woke up. Many times, they were very clear dreams that lingered with me for several minutes after I wake up in the morning. They even come at three o'clock in the morning and I would be fully awake. I would write them down on my journal and they will keep me thinking the following day. This very clear thought of "GOD'S FINGER-PRINTS" is one of them and happened on my 65th birthday. I know I ought to write this one book. I thought I was pursuing God all my life, even as I was building my business. Then I realized it was Him pursuing me all along, and I kept on running away. That was when I was younger. But as I grew older, I get to enjoy His call, His words, His visitations, His revelations, His pursuit of me, and my responding and pursuit of Him too. It was like a hide and seek process. It was a love affair. As I grew older, it became intensely personal, experiential, not an academic knowledge thing like what I had when I was younger. Believe me or not, God still speaks to us like He spoke to His prophets, His people, His friends, His children in the scriptures.

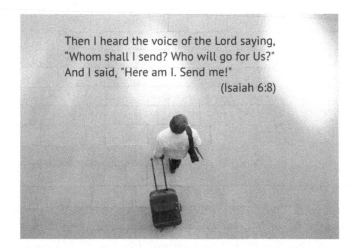

Then I heard the voice of the Lord saying, "Whom shall I send? Who will go for Us?" And I said, "Here am I. Send me!"
(Isaiah 6:8)

Then I heard the voice of the Lord saying, "Whom shall I send? Who will go for Us?" And I said, "Here am I. Send me!" (Isaiah 6:8)

———

My Heart's Response

Dear God, I am answering your call to write. But I don't want to write just anything. I want to write what you want to say to your people. So you will have to back me up along the way. I will wait for your inspiration. I will look back and find your fingerprints in the timeline of my life. I will feel your hands and see how you are holding me in this present time. I will look at where your fingers are pointing to guide my direction towards the future that you have set for me. I love you, and I thank you for everything.

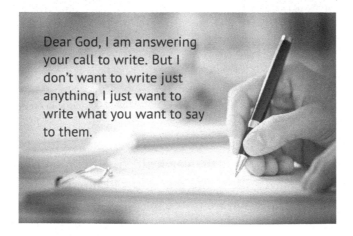

Dear God, I am answering your call to write. But I don't want to write just anything. I just want to write what you want to say to them.

———

God Is Touching You

And to you my reader, if you spend time meditating on these pages I wrote, and if you pray sincerely to God who inspired me to write these pages, you will experience His nearness, His presence and His love. You will be transformed and you will walk this earth seeing His fingerprints in the circumstances of your own life, in the lives of people around you, in the events of history. You will see that the story of this world is unfolding according to His plan and you are a part of it. The timeline of history of mankind is filled with the fingerprints of God as his hands works the fulfillment of His design in my life, in your life, in all of mankind and the created universe.

For the earth will be filled with the knowledge of the glory of the LORD as the waters cover the sea. (Habakkuk 2:14)

God is filling the earth with the knowledge of His glory. If you look at the globe, you see the earth filled with water. And if you could only see the depth of the sea, you will discover that there is no space in the entire surface of the depth of the sea not filled with water. As you keep reading, the depth of your mind, heart, and soul will be flooded by the knowledge of the glory of the Lord.

I pray that God will open the eyes of my spirit and yours to His glory that is being revealed and that we may both follow the leading of the Holy Spirit as I write this book and as you and I journey into the path of God's inspiration where we both will see His fingerprints and experience His presence.

For those who are led by the Spirit of God are the children of God. (Romans 8:14)

———

Speak To God In Your Heart

Imagine being like one of the two men whom Jesus appeared to on the road to Emmaus. They did not recognize him as Jesus spoke to them. Imagine all the times Jesus tried to speak to you through a book, a sermon, an encouraging word of a friend, a convincing word from someone. Think of all the times you did not recognize Him in your life as He tried to communicate with you.

> *Behold, I stand at the door and knock. If anyone hears my voice and opens the door, I will come in to him and eat with him, and he with me.* (Rev 3:20 ESV)

Now, you close your eyes and speak to God silently. He has been waiting for you for so long. Give Him time to speak to your heart too. In the beginning, this will be hard because our brain does not stop thinking. We have lost the art of listening. We cannot stand still. And yet God says,

> *"Be still and know that I am God."* (Psalm 46:10)

> *"Come now, let us reason together, says the Lord."* (Isaiah 1:18)

Do not hurry. Do not worry. Clear your mind of all concerns. Think of an imaginary box and imagine all your concerns as written on a piece of paper and locked inside that box, and you will pay attention to it again later. You might be surprised by the time you come back to them that they are not as important as you thought they were. You are in the presence of the God of the universe who created you because He loves you. Ask Him to make you understand and experience His love. Without knowing and experiencing His love, you cannot love Him. You can only think about Him, but not love Him. Your mind knows Him intellectually, but your heart is dry of love. Find Him in your spirit where He dwells. He is not in a building. I mean the consciousness of His love is not in a building. He is inside of you, in your consciousness. Of course, He is in the building because there is nothing where He is not present. What I mean is that His presence becomes so real to you only when you become aware of His presence in your spirit. That is where you and God meet and you become one with God. Stay on that awareness.

"Here I am! I stand at the door and knock. If anyone hears my voice and opens the door, I will come in and eat with that person, and they with me." (Revelation 3:20)

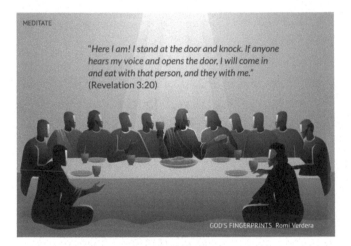

Yes, Jesus will eat with you. Did you not know he likes to eat with his friends. Not just eat but drink a little wine. He is happy. He celebrates. He wants to share his happiness with his friends. I bet you there was so much good food at the wedding in Cana where he performed his first miracle of changing water into wine. Good food and good wine. You would have loved to be there. He is a happy guy you know. You might have seen picture of him agonizing for carrying that heavy cross and being crucified. But he was suffering joyfully because he was doing it for you. Thank him for what he has done for you.

———

Chapter Three

HOW TO USE THIS BOOK

*"In the last days, God says, I will pour out my
Spirit on all people."* (Acts 2:17)

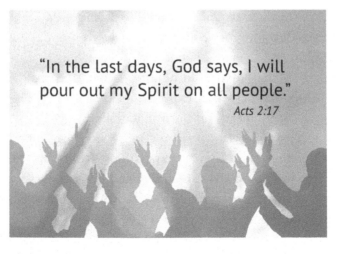

Each Chapter Have Four Sections
1st Section is how God touched me.
2nd Section: My Heart's Response

3rd Section: God is Touching You
4th Section: Speak To God In Your Heart

––––––

God Touched Me

I felt I was being electrocuted for a few moments as I was praying. I never thought before then that an experience like that can
ever happen to anyone on this planet earth. I saw a vision of cloud
and a bright white light shining behind it. Then I saw myself, a tiny
little dot of myself thrown into that bright light. I do not know
how I knew that the tiny little dot was myself being thrown and
engulfed by that light behind the bright cloud. Then I heard a still
small voice say, "You belong to me." Then I was in complete peace
and joy. It actually lasted for about two weeks, that feeling of
delight, peace and joy. It was a feeling of total carelessness for
anything except being with God. I did not care about all my problems. I had lots of them at that time. Later, everything that was
happening in the circumstances of my life day after day, month after
month, year after year, proved to me that heaven opened up to me
and a new life had begun. That was just the door. It was just the
beginning of another chapter in my life. What I just told you does
not give justice to the actual experience. It is so beyond descrip-
tion. You will not understand until it happens to you. I found out
later and through the years from people who have experienced a
similar happening that they always differ from one person to
another. This happened after an all-day church seminar that led me
to a prayer of surrendering my life to God that evening. As I was
praying my surrender to God, this heavenly experience happened.
My life was transformed after that. Reading the Bible was no longer
the same. I could feel the depth of what God meant for the people
in the Bible and for me. I am in it and its stories. I share the lives,
feelings, agony, doubts, struggle, and faith of the people of God.
Later, experiences taught me that healings are real, miracles are

real, and God's loving presence is real in myself and many people I met later in life. Since then up to this date, the words of Jesus reveals to me a new kind of depth each time I read them, sometimes, so mind-blowing different than my former understanding. It was like what he meant was hidden from me all these years. I could sense God breaking through into my life and into peoples' lives. Throughout the years, my thirst for God continues to deepen. He seems to fill us with His Holy Spirit to quench the thirst for a moment but then He wants us to long for Him all the time so this feeling of being filled is intensely momentary but subtly permanent. This section of the book contains the stories of these encounters, insights, and inspiration from God. I invite you to join me in my recollection of it. It will serve as a pathway for your own journey to the presence of God. Even I have to retrace and recollect my own experiences so I can find my way back to these beautiful moments of deep prayer encounter. I cannot bring you to the presence of God. You alone can do that for yourself. God is sovereign. God is God and we are not. I can only show you how by being thirsty, you are disposing yourself to His touch. It is Him who will lift you up to His glorious presence from where you've been stuck, a place in your prayer life you thought could not advance anymore.

———

My Heart's Response.

The recollection of God's touch and the experience of his presence always evoke a response of gratitude and love within me. On this section of the chapter, I pray my heart out. I enjoin you to pray with me. As you experience praying, your heart's longing for the touch of His presence will intensify.

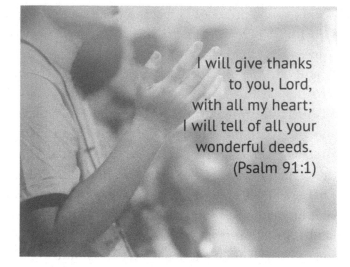

I will give thanks to you, Lord, with all my heart; I will tell of all your wonderful deeds. (Psalm 91:1)

———

God Is Touching You

The fact that you are reading this, He is touching you already. I am referring to what, sometimes, becomes an intense touch. I do not know when God will touch you that way. Maybe He will touch your heart while you are reading, or praying, or pondering. You will not ask whether He touched you or not because you will knqw for sure. He might touch you as you are reading this book. Maybe He might touch you later on after you read. Or maybe when you are totally doing something else and you are not even thinking of Him. He might even wake you up from your sleep. He does that to me many times, and I would be so wide awake and I would write what He told me on my journal.

In this section of the book, I will share with you some insights. Use them as stepping stones to your meditation of Him and His touches. Always remember that your goal is not to keep on reading so that you will know more. Your goal for reading is to lead you on the path to His presence. When you feel His presence, you should stop reading and just stay in His presence.

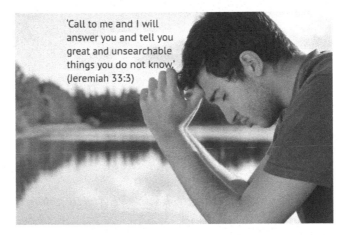

'Call to me and I will answer you and tell you great and unsearchable things you do not know.' (Jeremiah 33:3)

'Call to me and I will answer you and tell you great and unsearchable things you do not know.' (Jeremiah 33:3)

———

Speak To God In Your Heart

Always take a break and simply recollect your mind into His presence. Always remember, you are in His holy presence at all times. Our challenge is that our mind cannot keep still. One way to keep it still is by focusing your mind on a scripture passage. But do not stress yourself out. Practice relaxingly focusing on a simple phrase or even just a word, or a thought. Speak to God about your desire for His presence and love. Know that he knows your concerns even before you ask him for answers to your problems. You do not have to say much or repeat your petitions about mundane necessities. The thought of them many times takes you away from His presence. Always bring yourself back to your eagerness to be in His presence. In His presence, your concerns will melt in a miraculous way.

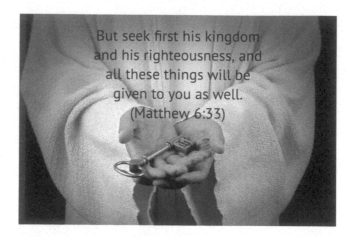

But seek first his kingdom and his righteousness, and all these things will be given to you as well. (Matthew 6:33)

———

Chapter Four

COMPANIONS ON THE ROAD

They asked each other, "Were not our hearts burning within us while he talked with us on the road and opened the Scriptures to us?" (Luke 24:32)

God Touched Me

In these pages, I will speak to God and hear from Him; I will speak to you and I will pray. I will share with you how God touched me and you will see His fingerprints. As you read these pages, God will touch you too and as you feel His touch, you too will speak to

God and pray. At the end of the day, we will see the fingerprints of God in every moment of the day, every words I wrote, everything I thought, the thoughts that comes to your mind, the feelings that you experience. God is not someone we just think about but someone who is with us whom we can experience and speak to. I ask for the gift of His spirit and I believe He honors our sincere prayers asking for His Holy Spirit.

> *If you then, though you are evil know how to give good gifts to your children, how much more will your Father in heaven give the Holy Spirit to those who ask him. (Luke 11:13)*

At the end of the day, you and I will be like the two men who walked with Jesus on the road to Emmaus after He resurrected from the grave. They, at first, did not recognize it was Jesus who was walking and talking with them on the road. They thought they were just talking about Jesus. At the end of the day when it was getting dark, they invited the man to stay with them for the evening. And this was what happened:

> *When he was at the table with them, he took bread, gave thanks, broke it and began to give it to them. Then their eyes were opened and they recognized him, and he disappeared from their sight. They asked each other, "Were not our hearts burning within us while he talked with us on the road and opened the Scriptures to us?" (Luke 24:30-32)*

This is what will happen as we experience being with Him in these meditations. Our hearts will burn as He speaks to us on the road of our mind and heart, and our hearts will burn as we read the Scriptures He leads us to.

————

My Heart's Response

Dear God, I sometimes look at what I am writing and I can't

see the connections, or the arrangement of thoughts to come out as a one whole beautiful picture. Let me always go back to the awareness that I only want to write what you say to my mind and that I should prayerfully wait for your inspiration. Lead me to what I should write. Jesus spent so much time in the evenings communing with you that is why He says He only speaks what He hears from you.

Fill my mind with your thoughts, my heart with your love, and my soul with your Holy Spirit. Lord, guide my fingers with your hands that you may have your fingerprints in these papers I am writing. Amen.

———

God Is Touching You

God wants to pour the fire of His spirit into your heart. He wants to open your eyes of faith. He wants you to hear His voice with the ears of your heart.

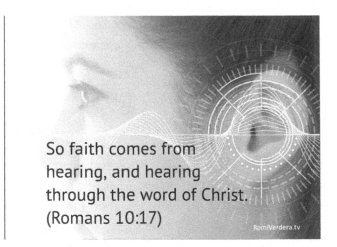

So faith comes from hearing, and hearing through the word of Christ. (Romans 10:17 ESV)

Allow Him to touch you. Be still. Your eyes of faith will open and you will see the spiritual realm behind this worldly realm that veils the workings of God. When you become aware of the workings of the hands of God on every little event that happens in this world, you will see His fingerprints more and more in your life, in the life of others, and in what is happening in the world. Meditate on the word of God that touches your heart and mind.

Your faith will increase as you read the word of God though the Gospel of Christ. Later, whenever you can, pick up a Bible and read the Gospel. Read the Gospels first. The books of the Old Testament all points to Christ and they will have meaning for you when you know Christ in the Gospels. Everyday, make a habit of reading the Scripture. It will make your awareness of God's presence in every moment of your life. And if you live in God's presence everyday, you will be at peace because you are experiencing living under the shadow of his wings. You are living in the kingdom that Jesus says is near and among us.

> *Being asked by the Pharisees when the kingdom of God would come, he answered them, "The kingdom of God is not coming in ways that can be observed, nor will they say, 'Look, here it is!' or 'There!' for behold, the kingdom of God is in the midst of you." (Luke 17:20-21 ESV)*

———

Speak To God In Your Heart

Be still. Put yourself in the presence of God. Quiet your mind. From what you have just read, focus on a phrase, a sentence, or a paragraph that touched your mind and heart. There is always an insight that opens a door in your imagination that leads you to deeper understanding of God, His ways, His will, His presence. Thank God for his revelation of himself. Close your eyes and wait.

Learn how to be patient in silence and let God touch your heart and mind in His time and His way. His revelation does not always come the same way, nor the way you expect them to be, nor at a time you expect it to come. God is full of surprises. Be patient and just have a surrendered heart to His will. You may not understand how He works or might often question His timing, but for as long as you are surrendered to His will in a childlike trust that you simply rest at His bossom not caring whether He manifest or not, but just caring that He loves you all the time, you will be at peace.

You keep him in perfect peace whose mind is stayed on you because he trusts in you. (Isaiah 26:3 ESV)

You keep him in perfect peace whose mind is stayed on you because he trusts in you. (Isaiah 26:3 ESV)

———

Chapter Five

SECRET TREASURES

I will give you hidden treasures, riches stored in secret places, so that you may know that I am the Lord. (Isaiah 45:2-3)

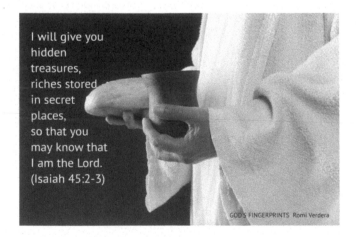

God Touched Me

What hidden treasures? Everything good. Wisdom, knowledge, guidance, love, insights, inspiration, gold nuggets for the soul, material provision, financial opportunity, job, business, prosperity, friends, loved ones, respect, and on and on, everything good because God is good. Be still and know that God is good. Ponder on it for several minutes. Your mind will be transformed and the word of God will become a reality in your life because the word of God is life.

———

My Heart's Response

Dear God, thank you for everything. You never fail to surprise me. These treasures are not really secrets. They are secret only because many times I take them for granted and I miss to recognize them as being from you. They are right before my eyes and yet I do not see it all the time. Always remind me that everything is from you so that I may always respond with love. I love you God. Amen.

> *Everything comes from the Lord. All things were made because of him and will return to him. Praise the Lord forever! Amen. (Romans 11:36 CEV)*

———

God Is Touching You

He is opening your eyes to his fingerprints. By fingerprints I mean His words, His moves, His actions in your life, the fulfillment of His design for human history. Nothing escapes Him.

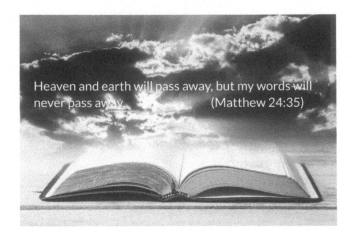

Heaven and earth will pass away, but my words will never pass away.
(Matthew 24:35)

Your ears are being opened to the sound of His voice. Your senses are becoming sensitive to the wind of His spirit. In His presence, there is no difference with the functions of your different faculties. There is just a "knowing" and you do not even understand how you knew it. Your soul would see and hear and yet your eyes might be close and you heard a sound but there was no sound. You just know that God communicated something to you.

Deep calls to deep in the roar of your waterfalls; all your waves and breakers have swept over me. (Psalm 42:7)

————

Speak To God In Your Heart
Be still. Put yourself in the presence of God. Be aware of your breathing until your mind becomes quiet. Express your gratitude for this gift of faith He is bestowing on you. He continues to reveal himself more and more to you. He is cementing the bond between Himself and you until your awareness of His presence remains with you every moment of the day. You could be working and doing

other things on your daily tasks but deep down in the recesses of your soul, you know He is there with you. Thank Him for a moment even while working for the knowledge of His presence. His providence will permeate every activity and project you are working on. Be still and ponder His presence. Thank Him for being with you.

For he performeth the thing that is appointed for me: and many such things are with him. (Job 23:14)

Chapter Six

THE NARROW GATE

"Enter through the narrow gate. For wide is the gate and broad is the road that leads to destruction, and many enter through it. But small is the gate and narrow the road that leads to life, and only a few find it." (Matthew 7:13-14)

God Touched Me

God's hand is on every moment of my life. He guides me on the right track as I walk on that narrow road, and He nudge me back to it in times when I get lost on the road and end on the wide road that leads to destruction. And yes, I fell on huge pot holes a few times that brought me so much misery then. And there were times I was hanging by the edge of that wide road leading to destruction. I dread the thought of what could have happened if God did not lift me up and brought me to the narrow road again. The hardest part then was that I brought misery to my own family, my wife, and my children in my old life. But that was decades ago. God restored me and my family. Today, my wife, my children, and grandchildren all learned to stay on the narrow road where God's peace, joy, and love is the atmosphere. This is the kingdom of God among us that Jesus speaks about.

"The kingdom of God is in your midst." (Luke 17:21)

For the kingdom of God is not a matter of eating and drinking, but of righteousness, peace and joy in the Holy Spirit. (Romans 14:17)

———

My Heart's Response

Dear God, my life could have been a nightmare had you not nudged me back into the narrow road. How could I have been so blind? Sometimes, I cannot grasp how I was so lost when I was younger. I see the old version of me and I wonder how ignorant and blind I was. Anyway, that's history. My consolation is that those ugly portions of my life make me very grateful today for the beauty of life lived in knowing you and experiencing your presence and love. Also, I am grateful for the privilege of being used by you to be a light to others undergoing the same circumstances of being lost in this chaotic world. I thank you God for everything. Thank you for loving me. I love you too, God. Amen.

———

God is Touching You

We are all on the road. Again, the fact that you are reading this book means, either you are on this narrow road and God wants to advance you closer to him; or you might be on the wide road and God is nudging you back on the narrow road. We all are born on the narrow road. When we were children, our hearts were pure. This narrow road of the kingdom of God belongs to children.

Jesus said, "Let the little children come to me, and do not hinder them, for the kingdom of heaven belongs to such as these." (Matthew 19:14)

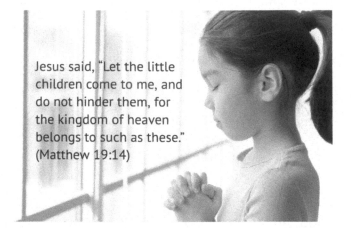

As we grow older, like a sponge, we absorb into our hearts and mind the contaminated waters of the world. Our hearts are hardened by those who hurt us. We become selfish as we live day by day for our own survival. We become cold to the needs of others. We lose our innocence.

Use your imagination and try to reflect on your life and examine where you might be on the road.

———

Speak To God In Your Heart

Ask God to show you to where you are on the road. Ask God to clear out of your way what hinders you from getting into His presence. It could be the tyranny of the demand of the present moment. It could be a repeated turning the other way around because of a weakness you need to conquer. Many times, we do not know how to free ourselves from the yokes that we carry on the road. We say that we have no option. Do not be discouraged. God loves you, no matter what. Stay in His love. He will guide you.

> *"Come to me, all you who are weary and burdened, and I will give you rest. Take my yoke upon you and learn from me, for I am gentle and humble in heart, and you will find rest for your souls. For my yoke is easy and my burden is light." (Matthew 11:28-30)*

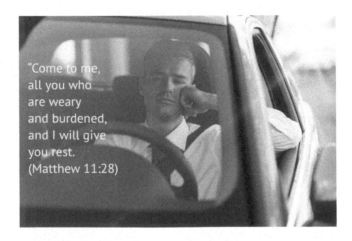

Chapter Seven

BE STILL AND KNOW

He says, "Be still, and know that I am God. I will be exalted among the nations. I will be exalted in the earth." (Psalm 46:10)

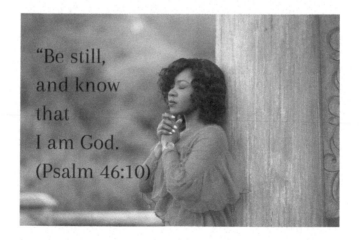

God Touched Me

I had to practice keeping my mind still because God said so. Our mind is like a wild horse that is so hard to tame. As soon as I wake up, it runs and runs. It thinks of problems, conversations, happenings, things that it fears. Every morning, I remind myself that I do not want to think of anything but God first. So what about God? What should I think about God? No, that's not it. I am not to think about God. I am to face God in my thinking. It's like when I am with my wife, I do not need to think about my wife. I face my wife and talk to her, hug her, love her. Many a times, we just keep quiet with each other like when we hang out by the beach chairs under the big umbrella. We are just together. It's the same thing with God. I do not have to find ways to think about God like read a book because God is there with me. So I just keep silent in my awareness that He is with me and I wait.

These words I am writing now came from Him. He led me to write this. I just woke up, and as usual, I keep my mind empty of any other thought that wants to creep into my mind in the morning. If ever I read a book, it is supposed to lead me to the awareness that God is with me. I cannot just keeping reading a book helping me think "about God." I want to be with God and I want Him to be near me so I could talk to Him face to face. For that to happen, I need to lay down the book and stop reading about God. Even from reading the Bible. I would read and allow the thoughts about what I read to bring me to the presence of God like riding a boat that brings me to the other side of the river. Like this morning, on that moment of quiet where I just sat there with God and wait. In the nothingness of thought came in His words, "Whatsoever things are true, have your mind in them." So God led me to that thought this morning; then, I went back to the Bible to see the entire message from God and kept my mind in it. I did not struggle to think "about God." God came to me and led me to what I should think about. This requires a lifetime of practice because the mind is so stubborn when it comes to keeping still.

"Whatever is true, whatever is noble, whatever is right, whatever is pure, whatever is lovely, whatever is admirable—if anything is excellent or praiseworthy—think about such things." (Philippians 4:8)

Think about such things

"Whatever is true,
whatever is noble,
whatever is right,
whatever is pure,
whatever is lovely,
whatever is admirable—
if anything is excellent or
praiseworthy—
think about such things."
(Philippians 4:8)

By the way, I slept at 12 midnight and was awakened at 5:30 am. I always try to sleep for eight hours, seven, at least. But this morning at 5:30am, I only had five-and-a-half of sleep so far. I could have made myself go back to bed and sleep until 7 or 8am, but I just stood up and washed my face and went downstairs to our dining table where I do my writing because God wanted me to write this already.

———

My Heart's Response

Dear God, thank you for waking me up. I will just make up for my sleep later. Or maybe you would just keep me up strong without even needing to make up for my sleep. I love these mornings where my head is so clear and my spirit is attuned to your Spirit. My heart too is bubbling with joy. I pray for all who will read this. May you guide them to your presence and may they experience the joy of being in your presence. Amen.

This is the day the Lord has made; let us rejoice and be glad in it. (Psalm 118:24)

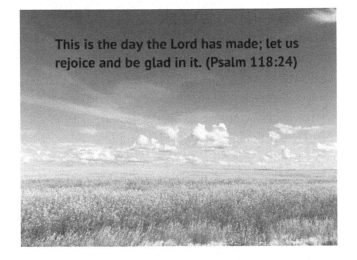

This is the day the Lord has made; let us rejoice and be glad in it. (Psalm 118:24)

God Is Touching You

He wants you to be still. This might be hard in the beginning. Learn to be still for a minute, then two, then three, then as long as you can be still in His presence. Do not think of your thoughts about God. Just be aware of His presence around you and in you. He knows every bit of thought you are thinking even before you think of Him. He is aware of every feeling you have, your concerns, your hesitations, your anxieties, even your deepest subconscious fears that you are not even conscious of. Just give them all to Him and be still.

Speak To Him In Your Heart

Tell him, "I love you God." Did you ever love anybody? Think of the person you love the most. Then now desire that you love God more than that person. God ought to be your number one love because he even gave you all the persons that you love and that love you. And if you can't find in your heart anybody whom you really love and anybody who really loves you, that's alright. God loves you more than you love yourself. And even if you think you do not love yourself, God loves you, that is why He created you and He wants you to not just try to believe it, but He wants you to feel and experience it in your heart. You might have to quiet your brain for this because your brain wants to analyze everything including your own heart. Let your heart be free. Say inside of you, "I love you God." If you can say it with your lips, you have made a giant leap. Do not worry if you do not mean it yet. We all start with just "wanting to love God." Then God honors that desire of your heart and He pours His love into your heart. Then, one day, you begin to wonder why you "never felt this way before." You find yourself really loving God.

God's love has been poured out into our hearts through the Holy Spirit, who has been given to us. (Romans 5:5)

God's love has been poured out into our hearts through the Holy Spirit, who has been given to us. (Romans 5:5)

Chapter Eight

DISCIPLINE SEEMS PAINFUL

For the moment all discipline seems painful rather than pleasant, but later it yields the peaceful fruit of righteousness to those who have been trained by it. (Hebrews 12:11, ESV)

For the moment all discipline seems painful rather than pleasant, but later it yields the peaceful fruit of righteousness to those who have been trained by it. (Hebrews 12:11, ESV)

God Touched Me

I look back at my life and I see God's fingerprints in those grueling moments of negative life events called adversity. I look back and I see how He built my obstacle course to train my legs so I can run faster. He expanded my lungs so I can breathe deeper and fight longer. He hardened my muscles so I can carry the sword and the shield, so that I can swing it to the enemy, the devil, when he attacks me.

Therefore put on the full armor of God, so that when the day of evil comes, you may be able to stand your ground, and after you have done everything, to stand. (Ephesians 6:13)

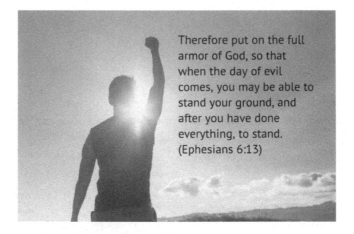

Therefore put on the full armor of God, so that when the day of evil comes, you may be able to stand your ground, and after you have done everything, to stand. (Ephesians 6:13)

My soul is filled with the fire of the Holy Spirit expanding the kingdom of God in every corner of my life and extending God's reign into the hearts of other men that get near me. I do not worry who might read this book or not. It is God who makes me write and it is God who knows to whom He is making me write this for. He is building His army and He is building it through His word and His spirit.

———

My Heart's Response

Dear God, I am so grateful for your generosity in giving me a chance to serve in your army. I thank you for all those times I thought I was being crushed when the reality is that I was being trained in your boot camp. Now, I see that it was a must that I needed to go through so that I can be used for training others too. Amen.

———

God is Touching You

Look back at your life and you will see that there are lessons learned for every crisis you went through. Each adversity is an invitation by God to let Him into your life. It is not that God wants you to suffer. His perfect will is that we live in a continuous enjoyment of His presence in which all negative aspects of life melt away. But we are in this world still in which His kingdom is, and is not yet. His kingdom reigns in your life when you become aware of His love, His presence, His mercy, His forgiveness, His joy, and you do not just think about it but really experience it. In the absence of this awareness and experience, you are only aware of the processes by which life events around you are happening. And somehow, many a times, there seems to be no sense to this flow of events. When you do not see the big picture, you wonder if there is any meaning to it all. All you see are the struggle and suffering in human living and the seasons of relief. And maybe success, which most often, do not last. And if success last longer, it might be just in one area of life at the expense of another area. Only when life is lived in the perfect will of God that all miseries melt away. For most, it is a lifetime journey and will find its completion when we see Him face to face. For those who find the reign of God in their heart in this world, the beginning of that "kingdom of God life" where peace, joy, and love pour out like in a fountain starts here on this earth.

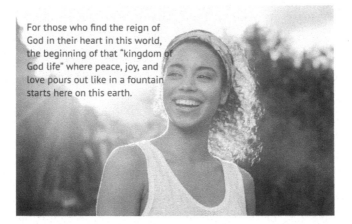

For those who find the reign of God in their heart in this world, the beginning of that "kingdom of God life" where peace, joy, and love pours out like in a fountain starts here on this earth.

"The time has come," he said. "The kingdom of God has come near. Repent and believe the good news!" (Mark 1:15)

Speak To God In Your Heart

We often come to God only when we need Him to remedy some bad happenings in our lives. No one is exempt from suffering, from undergoing some seasons of brokenness. But the solution to these negative experiences are less important than the experience of God's nearness. It results from us trying to find God, and His power and love, as a way of solving our problems. Speak to God in your heart and let Him know that it is Him that you want. It takes a renewing of mind to lift God in our awareness instead of the things we want from God. Most times, our mind is hypnotized by the things of this earth that we are asking God for. We always lose sight of the fact that if we can only keep our mind in God, and His power and love, all things will be well because He will fight our battles for us. Focus on Him! Meditate on this thought over and over again until a shift in your mind happens from thinking about your problem to thinking about God, His power, and His love.

But seek first his kingdom and his righteousness, and all these things will be given to you as well. (Matthew 6:33)

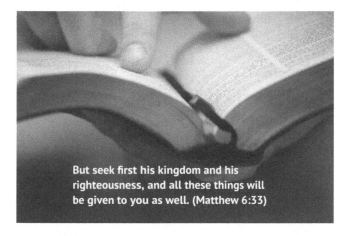

But seek first his kingdom and his righteousness, and all these things will be given to you as well. (Matthew 6:33)

Chapter Nine

HE IS ALL OVER ME

You have searched me, Lord, and you know me. You know when I sit and when I rise; you perceive my thoughts from afar. (Psalm 139:1-2)

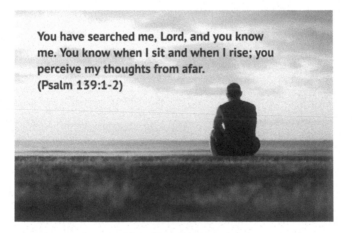

You have searched me, Lord, and you know me. You know when I sit and when I rise; you perceive my thoughts from afar. (Psalm 139:1-2)

God Touched Me

I look back and I see His fingerprints all over me. They are in my mind, heart and soul. He nudged me into the right directions at the crossroads of my life.

He was there when I married, divorced and remarried my wife.

He was there when my business was booming, when I went bankrupt and lost everything, and when I found a new business and my finances built up once more. He was there in the ups and downs of my life. He let me fall and He restored me. His hand was holding me in my darkest hour leading me back to the light.

Where can I go from your Spirit. Where can I flee from your presence? If I go up to the heavens, you are there; if I make my bed in the depths, you are there. (Psalm 139:7-8)

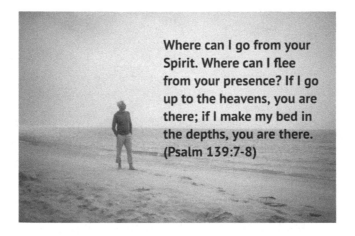

Where can I go from your Spirit. Where can I flee from your presence? If I go up to the heavens, you are there; if I make my bed in the depths, you are there. (Psalm 139:7-8)

I remember a time when I thought my life was like a broken glass, where I had no way of getting the pieces back together again. But I knew nothing was impossible to Him. He brought to life the dead man named Lazarus, commanded the storm to calm down, fed five thousand men, changed water to wine, made the blind to see, and rose Himself from the dead. So, I believed He could restore the broken pieces of my life back to wholeness and He did. That is why I am writing about recognizing His fingerprints in our lives. Because recognizing them gives us hope that He is real and believing in Him gives us hope in the healing power of His touch.

———

My Heart's Response

Dear God, nothing escapes Your knowledge. You knew me before the foundation of the world.

"My frame was not hidden from You when I was made in secret, when I was woven together in the depths of the earth. Your eyes saw my unformed body; all the days ordained for me were written in your book before one of them came to be." (Psalm 139:15-16)

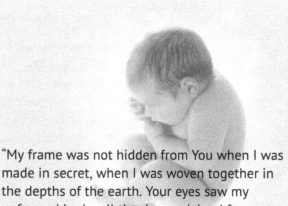

"My frame was not hidden from You when I was made in secret, when I was woven together in the depths of the earth. Your eyes saw my unformed body; all the days ordained for me were written in your book before one of them came to be." (Psalm 139:15-16)

You sustain in existence every atom of my body. You put Your breath in me. You put joy in my heart. You pick me up when I fall. You are my light in my darkest moments. I wait on You. I thirst for You like the deer longs for stream of water.

———

God Is Touching You

Find a quiet place. Sit down and clear your mind of any thought. Be mindful of your breathing to calm your mind. Imagine how you are made of. You are a gazillion miles of nerves. Starting from two cells that joined into one and kept on multiplying in your mother's womb, you started as a tiny little being that grew in nine months into a little baby. Your DNA determined how you would look like, the color of your hair, your likeness to your parents, how tall you would be. Your physical body is a miracle of creation. Your heart would beat about 42,000,000 times per year and would not stop from the time you were in the womb to your last breath. Your heart is a miracle. God not only knows every atom of your body but He also knows your thoughts before you think them. He designed and sustains your whole being. You are made up of the same elements as the stars in the sky which are billions of years old. Your brain is a most sophisticated computer capable of containing all the content of the internet in the whole world. There is not one moment that God is not thinking of you. He knows the number of the stars in the sky. You wonder how God could love you and you might sometime think that you are unlovable. That is because not even you know yourself. God knows you more than you know yourself. That is why God loves you more than anybody loves you and more than you love yourself. He understands your innermost thought and the reason why you think the way you think.

> God not only knows every atom of your body but he also knows your thoughts before you think them. He designed and sustains your whole being.

Speak To God In Your Heart

Be still. Clear your mind by focusing on your breathing until thoughts quiet down. Now, speak to God in the silence of your heart. Express your wonderment of His knowledge of you. Express your thankfulness for His love for you. If you do not feel love and gratitude, ask God to pour His grace of love and gratitude into you. You can not build or psyche yourself to love and gratitude. It is a result of your knowing and experiencing that He loves you first. Contemplation or your experience of union with God is something that you can not make happen to yourself. Unless God lifts your spirit up by His sovereign will, all your attempt at trying to commune with God is useless. You have to be so humble that it is Him alone who reveals Himself to us and all we can do is dispose and prepare ourselves for His touch of grace. You should constantly bring back your mind to the state of receptiveness to His touch. You will know when He touch you. You can not help but stay in His presence and you would not want to get out from there.

"Better is one day in your court than a thousand elsewhere..." (Psalm 84:10)

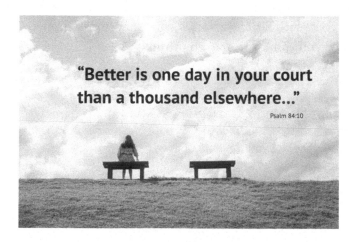

"Better is one day in your court than a thousand elsewhere..."
Psalm 84:10

Chapter Ten

TROUBLE INTERRUPTIONS

Call on me in the day of trouble; I will deliver you, and you will honor me. (Psalm 50:15)

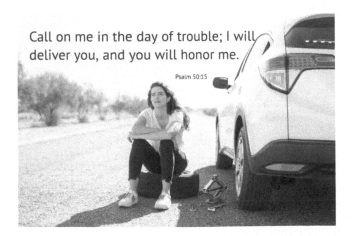

Call on me in the day of trouble; I will deliver you, and you will honor me.

Psalm 50:15

God Touched Me

Why should I thank God for a flat tire? We arrived in Cancun, Mexico for a two weeks' vacation. We reached the airport and took the shuttle bus to the rent-a-car place. Then we headed to the resort which is a half-an-hour drive. It was raining, and as I was driving, I saw a maybe a foot diameter pot hole full of water on the street. It was too late to avoid it, so I just drove through it. I felt a little bump. When we arrived at the front of the hotel, as my wife was checking-in at the lobby, I found out that we had a flat tire. Now that I am writing about flat tires, I tried to recall how many times I personally changed my own flat tire in my whole life. I can remember five times in the last fifty years. That is an average of one every ten years. The first one was I was vacationing in California with my wife and two little sons in my 20s and the tire blew up in the highway. Rent-a-cars always have the spare and tools in the trunk so I took them out and changed it. I don't think I thought of asking God's help at that time. Of course, I was upset why that had to happen during my fun vacation. I just took care of myself and changed the tires. The second one was in my early 30s. I just got out of the church from a whole day seminar about how God so loves us and I was so high on Jesus and as I was ready to drive home that evening and my tire was flat. Now, this is something. I just came out of a church having surrendered my life to Jesus experiencing the joy of my new found life learning that He cares for me and here I got a flat tire.

"Rejoice always, pray continually, give thanks in all circumstances; for this is God's will for you in Christ Jesus." (1 Thessalonians 5:18)

Then I learned much about flat tires after that. Flat tires are bad things that happen in our lives. It happens to everyone. No one is exempt for as long as we are in this world.

"In this world you will have trouble. But take heart! I have overcome the world." (John 16:33)

My job is to fix my flat tire. I can't do it alone. I need God's help even with a flat tire. He gives me air to breathe, to bring oxygen to my lungs, to supply energy to my bones and muscles, so I can do my job. He gives me joy and courage so I do not to have to be overcome by despair as I try to ease my situation. He gives me hope that everything will go well afterwards, and I will not have a flat tire again for the rest of my vacation.

The question is: "Did God will my flat tire, or did He just allow it to happen but it was not His will?" How could it be that God's will is in every circumstance that happens in my life? Is it His will for me to suffer, be miserable, agonize over my lot in life, be in crisis for the rest of my life? I tell you, NO.

> *For I know the plans I have for you," declares the Lord, "plans to prosper you and not to harm you, plans to give you hope and a future. (Jeremiah 29:11)*

So why do bad things happen to me then? I needed to find answers if I have to find some meaning out of things that happen in my life. I used to just accept the religious teaching that "our suffering is God's will so we should just accept them." Then I learned that many of us suffer not because it is God's perfect will, but because many of our sufferings are self-created. We may call it His "permissive will," but not His perfect will. There was a time I would often suffer chronic gout, a very painful inflammation on my feet and legs. Then I learned that it was because I used to drink so much beer and eat all kinds of salty junk chips. One time I did that on a vacation in the Caribbean and by halfway on the week of my vacation, I was limping from pain and I had to use a cane to walk. By the time we got back in New York, we got to our car in the airport parking lot, and I could not bend my knee anymore and the pain was excruciating. That was the first time I experienced I could not bend my knee, and I was in so much pain. I had to sit at the back seat of the car with my knee straight. One little movement and my whole body gets electrocuted with pain. I had to let my wife drive us back home. That was the last time I ever drank beer and ate salty junk potato chips. This was not the first time these things caused me pain. But this day was the worst.

"The thief comes only to steal and kill and destroy; I have come that they may have life, and have it to the full." (John 10:10)

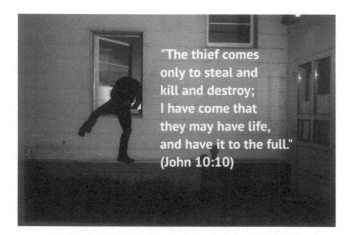

Yes, the enemy the devil comes to steal our health, finances, joy, happiness, peace, fun, family, friends, and all others that we value in life, while Jesus says He came that we may have life to the full.

But there are sickness or situations that we get into, not because of our own doing, but because we are connected to a whole network of lives that is not in our control. God had allowed us to be part of them. We do not always see the whole picture.

His disciples asked Him, "Rabbi, who sinned, this man or his parents, that he was born blind?" "Neither this man nor his parents sinned," said Jesus, "but this happened so that the works of God might be displayed in him. (John 9:3)

I could go on and on with this thread on "God's permissive will" and "God's perfect will." In any case, I believe that God's will for our life here on earth is for us to strive to be "as it is in heaven," as Jesus taught us to ask the Father.

———

My Heart's Response

Dear God, I am no different than most people. I too, ask where are you every time some real bad thing happens. Why did you allow it to happen? Thank you for giving me the grace to understand that I will never understand everything fully. Many times it is enough that I understand that no matter what, you are still a loving God and only you know all the angles to every story. And at any point in time, I should understand that the story is not finished yet. Every time I would think that the story has come to an end and that the ending of the story is horrible, I should come to a realization that it is not the end of the story yet.

I've seen it happen over and over in my own life, and in the life of others. What seemed to be so awful today will be of no consequence years later. What seemed to be a deadly painful wound today that make us cry, will one day be just a scar, and we can laugh about it.

I pray that you fill my mind with wisdom, understanding of your power and love, and that you are always way ahead of me into my own future.

"...I go and prepare a place for you..." (John 14:3)

———

God Is Touching You

In a quiet place, ponder these things. Practice relaxing and clearing your mind of thoughts. Your mind is like a wild horse sometimes. It would not stop thinking. The way you keep it quiet is you engage yourself in some sense exercise, like listening to a particular sound around you.

Imagine God lovingly watching you as you were developing in your mother's womb. He had put together the story of your life from beginning to end. But of course, He has allowed room for your exercise of your freewill. You have to freely choose to act within His will if you are to enjoy the fullness of living His abundant life. He had designed for every circumstance of your life to nudge you into the direction of fellowship with Him for all eternity. He knows all the pitfalls, the detours, the dangers, the turnarounds, the mistakes and the corrections, the damages and the restorations that will be on the way. He knows the road is not smooth, and most often, not straight but He improvised means for your safe passage. He has assigned angels to help you. He has placed people around you to help you stay on course. Best of all, He has put His Spirit in you to guide you through on the journey.

Silently speak to God in your heart and thank Him. Also, ask His forgiveness for all the times you ignore His whispers through your intuition. He was speaking through your conscience. He was connecting through the good thoughts that are popping up in your mind.

Speak To God In Your Heart

Stay on the thought that He is near you watching and loving you. The more you practice being conscious of His presence and yourself being loved by Him, the easier it gets to transport yourself from the noise of this world to the realm of His presence. Then it is easy to response to His love because you are no longer disturbed by all the noises around you. You will have to learn how to make the truth in your mind lead your heart. Sometimes your mind leads your heart, and other times your heart leads your mind. There will be times when your heart would want your mind to be quiet so that it can function. God cannot be fully understood by the mind, but the heart can overflow with love of God . Know that you have a spirit in which the Spirit of God dwells. When your mind is quiet, and your heart loves, and your spirit is filled with the Holy Spirit of God, your spirit then leads your heart and mind and you live by the Spirit.

Speak to God in the silence of your heart. Ask God to fill you with His Holy Spirit.

My soul thirsts for God, for the living God. When can I go and meet with God? (Psalm 42:2)

———

Chapter Eleven

GOD'S AGENDA FOR ME AND YOU

"You knit me together in my mother's womb." (Psalm 139:13)

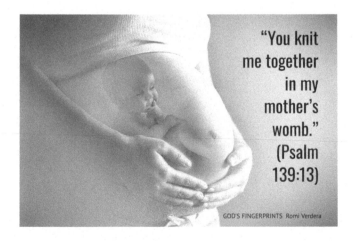

"You knit me together in my mother's womb." (Psalm 139:13)

GOD'S FINGERPRINTS Romi Verdera

God Touched Me

My 65th birthday was the first day of a new season of my life. That was the day i was inspired by God inspired me to spend the rest of my earthly life as a writer. Whether many people will read my books or not is immaterial. I am writing for God because it is him Him who gave me my breath all these years and on my 65th birthday. I woke up in the morning with an impression inside of me that says "God's Fingerprint." I knew it was supposed to be a book that I should write. I knew He was asking me to write it. I am writing for you because I know that's what God intended this writing to be. When I was a young man in school, I read a book by a man of God. The pages are nuggets of his wisdom about life. I thought one day I would write a book like him. I was a teenager then. Now I am 65 and I finally started writing. It took that long because I thought I was always young and did not have enough wisdom to write. Now, I do not have any excuse anymore. Jesus said that we should not hide the lamp under the table but put it up where the light could be seen. I want to be a light to people like Jesus says. I did not want to bury my talent in writing. I believe it is one of the talents God gave me. God forbid I don't use it and when I see Him face to face, I would have no answer as to why I did not use it. You all know what happened to the servant who buried his talents. I don't want to be like that. So here's the first light i I want to share with you: " Do not bury your talent. Let your light shine before men." Do not be afraid of what anybody would say. Just care of what God would say. One day you will see Him face to face. You will, you know.

My Heart's Response

Dear God, I pray that you equip me with wisdom to see Your design in my life, that I may run with all cylinders the way You constructed me. I know I am not here just for myself. I am here to be part of Your crew in building your kingdom on earth. May I recognize the talents You have given me so that I may develop them to the full for Your glory. Lead me to the right people who can help me. And lead me to the right people you You intend for me to help. Just as You Father has given to Jesus the disciples for Him to guide, I pray that You enable me to be aware of the people around me whom You want me to lead to You. Amen.

————

God Is Touching You

Imagine yourself being formed in the mind of God even before the creation of the world.

"...he chose us in him before the creation of the world..." (Ephesians 1:4)

Wow, before the creation of the world. That was a long time before you were born. Imagine God planning every event of your whole life long before He formed you in your mother's womb. He was loving you as He was forming you day by day in your mother's womb.

"Your eyes saw my unformed body; all the days ordained for me were written in your book before one of them came to be." (Psalm 139:16)

Imagine God putting together a good plan, a destiny for you. You are not an accident. You are loved.

For I know the plans I have for you," declares the Lord, "plans to prosper you and not to harm you, plans to give you hope and a future. (Jeremiah 29:11)

> For I know the plans I have for you,"
> declares the Lord, "plans to prosper
> you and not to harm you, plans to
> give you hope and a future.
>
> *Jeremiah 29:11*

Speak To God In Your Heart

God does not have any other agenda for creating you except to share his His life and love with you. Keep your mind on the awareness that He has loved you from the beginning of time. He has loved you and continues to love you today, and will love you forever. He is love. His power, might, and knowledge, are all in the service of love for you. Keep your mind on the knowledge of his His love until that knowledge permeates into your heart, and your heart responds with love. Utter the response of your heart in an audible whisper on your lips. Listen to your heart's expression coming out of your lips of your love response to God.

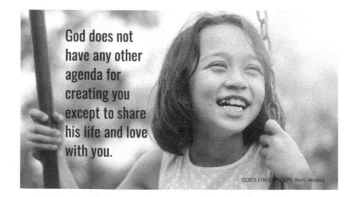

God does not have any other agenda for creating you except to share his life and love with you.

GOD'S FINGERPRINTS Romi Verdera

Open my lips, Lord, and my mouth will declare your praise. (Psalm 51:15)

———

Chapter Twelve

IT IS GOD COMMUNICATING

If any of you lacks wisdom, you should ask God, who gives generously to all without finding fault, and it will be given to you. (James 1:5)

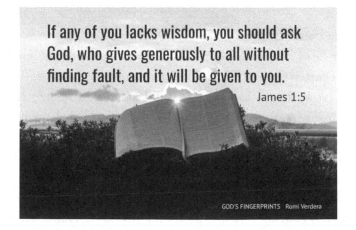

If any of you lacks wisdom, you should ask God, who gives generously to all without finding fault, and it will be given to you.

James 1:5

GOD'S FINGERPRINTS Romi Verdera

God Touched Me

I am trying to communicate with you. But when I come to think of it, it really is God attempting to communicate with you through me. Many times I would find myself talking to God, saying, "Lord, if You do not tell me what to say to them, I have nothing to write." Sometimes it would take me so long to wait, and at other times, I would just be flowing with the movement of the inspiration. The thing is, when they come so fast, I could not write them fast enough. So I use a voice recording machine, and I record the thoughts first, and then transcribe it later. Of course, I know there is no new revelation. God simply draws from my inner mind what He had deposited there all along my entire life.

Inside of me there is a lifetime of ideas, experiences, and pieces of a giant puzzle of my life, that God simply rearranges and uses as a way of communicating His message to you. If you find yourself agreeing with what I wrote, that is because God has placed the same thought in my book inside of you, even before you read my book. And He is just reminding you of something you actually already know. You are just being awakened from your sleep. God is just opening your eyes and sharpening your spiritual ear to hear, so that you can discover what is inside of you.

—————

My Heart's Response

Dear God, there was a time when there were so much junks inside of me, wrong ideas and bad experiences that messed me up so bad. Now that I look back, I did not even realize then how messed up my mind was, and how much emotional turmoil I was undergoing. How could I have been so wrong. ? I was so clueless as to about what was happening to me. But then one day I felt You. You broke into my mind and heart as if a light shone into my dark life, and I started to experience Your wonderful love and mercy.

I started praying to you You for my life to be transformed, from a life imprisoned to the miseries of this earth, to a life "as it is in heaven." I thank you You God, for opening my eyes to see that there is another life awaiting for me to discover. I began to understand Jesus' word, "I am the life." I found out I was dead and had no life. I was just going thru the motion of eating, drinking, working and having fun, I thought. The truth was, I had no life apart from You. I am grateful for my life now with You. Amen.

"I am the way and the truth and the life...." (John 14:6)

———

God Is Touching You

He wants you to look back into your life and recall the moments you felt loved, no matter how faint the memory would be. What blocks people from understanding the love of God is the absence of the feeling of having been loved. Many people can recall a lot of how someone got angry at them, or someone rejected them, or someone ignored them. And in case you can not cannot remember a time when you were loved, ask God to give you an experience of being loved by Him and stay quiet and wait. Be patient. He loves you.

The problem with many of us is that we cannot stay still. We are incapable of receiving that love because of emotional filters that block the entrance of the movement of this love in our hearts. Our hearts have become hardened with layers and layers of rejection embedded in our experience. And until His love gets through to us, we will not love him back.

But God demonstrates his own love for us in this: While we were still sinners, Christ died for us. (Romans 5:8)

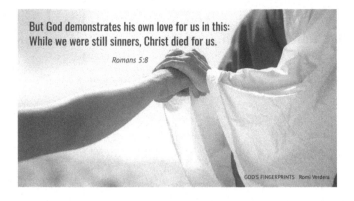

But God demonstrates his own love for us in this: While we were still sinners, Christ died for us.

Romans 5:8

GOD'S FINGERPRINTS Romi Verdera

Speak To God In Your Heart

Be still. Quiet your mind. Meditate on God watching you lovingly. I think most people got it wrong, thinking that God loves only the good people. God loves the good and the bad just as the sunshine falls on both of them. This is the reason why Jesus asked us not to judge. That includes not judging ourselves wrongly.

Everything is a gift from God, and even a person's goodness is a gift, so no one can boast. Speak to God and thank him for loving you unconditionally. Ask God's forgiveness for the times you judged yourself as not worthy of God's love, and you judged others the same way.

"I have loved you, my people, with an everlasting love. With unfailing love I have drawn you to myself." (Jeremiah 31:3)

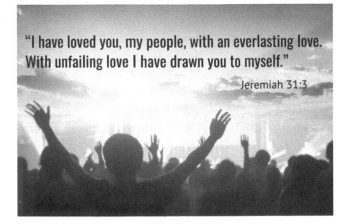

"I have loved you, my people, with an everlasting love. With unfailing love I have drawn you to myself."

Jeremiah 31:3

Chapter Thirteen

DO NOT WORRY

But I will sing of your strength, in the morning I will sing of your love, for you are my fortress, my refuge in times of trouble. (Psalm 59:16)

But I will sing of your strength, in the morning I will sing of your love, for you are my fortress, my refuge in times of trouble.

Psalm 59:16

God Touched Me

Jesus says sufficient is the trouble for today and tomorrow will worry about itself. Today our rental car had a flat tire. That's enough trouble for me for the day. It's been a long time I changed a flat tire myself. We returned to the rental place driving with the spare tube tire. They installed a new tire. Trouble resolved for the day. Do I get big troubles? Of course, I do. One time I was vacationing in Florida and my accountant-lawyer in New York called me to tell me of a big trouble that needs my attention. After hearing the troubling news on the phone, I can still remember today clearly what I did.

I told God I am not ruining my week's vacation in Florida by worrying about it, so I am giving it to Him, and later I will deal with it when I come back to New York. When I got back to New York, that very unpleasant situation was solved miraculously. Even my lawyer said that the solution was a "chance of a lifetime." Well, God gave me the chance and my trouble resolved. God fixed it for me. I like Jesus' teachings on how to deal with life's troubles. He makes everything simple.

Therefore do not worry about tomorrow, for tomorrow will worry about itself. Each day has enough trouble of its own. (Matthew 6:34)

Therefore do not worry about tomorrow, for tomorrow will worry about itself. Each day has enough trouble of its own.
Matthew 6:34

See you tomorrow...

GOD'S FINGERPRINTS Romi Verdera

My Heart's Response

Dear God, thank you for all the times you You calmed the storms of my life. I can recall the many times I passed through the agonizing moments of my life and I cried to you, and you came to the my rescue. Many times my agonies were not the same as your agony in Calvary. Yours were an offering to the Father for our wrongs. My sufferings were because of my own wrongs. Thank you for suffering for my wrongs so that I could be saved from them. I love you Jesus.

But he was pierced for our transgressions, he was crushed for our iniquities, the punishment that brought us peace was on him, and by his wounds we are healed. (Isaiah 53:5)

————

God Is Touching You

Be still. Calm your mind. You are in God's presence. Dwell on that thought. I do not know what storm you are going through. Maybe you are in dire need of money. Maybe it's your agonizing relationship with someone you love. Maybe it is your health. Maybe you are anxious about the future. Maybe you are suffering from intellectual bankruptcy and emotional turmoil. Maybe you think you have everything in life and yet you are dissatisfied with everything and you feel a vacuum inside of you. God wants to fill you up, not just patch you up. Spend some quiet time with Him and allow Him to touch your heart. Memorize one phrase in the Gospel that touches you and keep meditating on it.

If you abide in me, and my words abide in you, ask whatever you wish, and it will be done for you. (John 15:7)

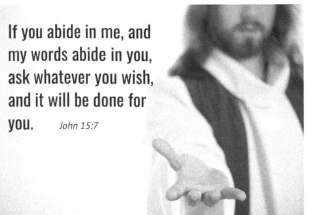

If you abide in me, and my words abide in you, ask whatever you wish, and it will be done for you. *John 15:7*

Speak To God In Your Heart

Give Jesus your life's storm. He is not sleeping. He is just waiting for you to ask him Him to calm it. Not that He does not know. But if He just does it, you will never know He did it. You have no idea many of your storms He just calmed for you, or He did not even let it come near you. Some He waits for you to ask him to calm. So he can be near you.

> *"Don't you believe that I am in the Father, and that the Father is in me? The words I say to you I do not speak on my own authority. Rather, it is the Father, living in me, who is doing his work." (John 14:10)*

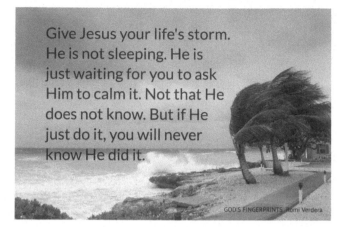

Give Jesus your life's storm. He is not sleeping. He is just waiting for you to ask Him to calm it. Not that He does not know. But if He just do it, you will never know He did it.

GOD'S FINGERPRINTS, Romi Verdera

Chapter Fourteen

LIFE IS A PERSON

Then Jesus declared, "I am the bread of life. Whoever comes to me will never go hungry, and whoever believes in me will never be thirsty. (John 6:35)

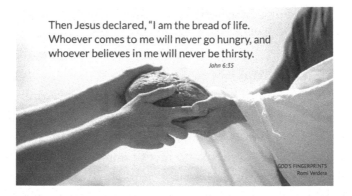

God Touched me

Do I have life? Is this life I am living now the life that Jesus is talking about? He says He is the life. This may sound confusing or something hard to grasp, but if I have no life, that is a big serious thing. I do not want to be a person with no life. That is boring. That is because we think we already know everything, and there is nothing more to life than what we already know. Life on this earth continues to eternity, and I do not want to have no life forever. That is a long long time to spend with not having life. So I want to make sure I have life now. So what is this life Jesus is talking about? It is Him. Jesus is life.

"Whoever has the Son has life; whoever does not have the Son of God does not have life."

1 John 5:12

———

My Heart's Response

My heart's response is gratitude for this supernatural life. It is a life that God wants me to enjoy on this earth and in the hereafter. It is a life lived in daily fellowship with Him. I am not alone on this earth. My God is my friend. That is life. Thank you God for letting me know and experience its reality. Amen.

———

God Is Touching You

Your life on this earth does not have to be a drab. God is inviting you to a more exciting life. Imagine yourself entering the earthly life. Once, you were a child full of curiosity of the world around you. You go to school and meet people. Then you grow into adulthood, work to survive, maybe build a family, pursue higher dreams, go through trials and tribulations, then maybe go through a season of identity crisis when you ask yourself, "Is this it? Is there more to life?" And as you grow older and older you come think of your own mortality. What is next?

The life of mortals is like grass, they flourish like a flower of the field; the wind blows over it and it is gone, and its place remembers it no more. (Psalm 103:15-16)

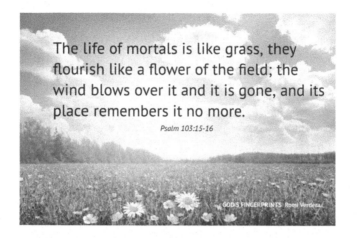

There is more to your life. That is why Jesus came, to show us the way to this new exciting life. He leads us to the narrow road that leads to life. While many people are lost in the wide road, the fact that you made it to this page of this book is that you are already on this narrow road. Follow Jesus.

Jesus answered, "I am the way and the truth and the life. No one comes to the Father except through me. (John 14:16)

Start forming the habit of reading Jesus' words in the Gospels. Reflect on the things He said. He does not waste words. Every bit of what He said will lead you to life with God. Taste the sweetness of His words.

"If you remain in me and my words remain in you, ask whatever you wish, and it will be done for you. This is to my Father's glory, that you bear much fruit, showing yourselves to be my disciples. As the Father has loved me, so have I loved you. Now remain in my love." (John 15:7-9)

"If you remain in me and my words remain in you, ask whatever you wish, and it will be done for you. *John 15:7*

GOD'S FINGERPRINTS Romi Verdera

———

Speak To God In Your Heart

Thank Him for choosing you. Yes, you are chosen. You are not a random product of creation. This might be hard for you to believe. But that is the truth. He made you in His image and likeness, and He breath His life into you. The reason why you might find this hard to believe is that instead of believing that God made you in His image, you tend to think of God as being in man's image and likeness, with a limited knowledge and love. No, He is not like that. He knows how many stars there are in the whole universe, and He knows how many atoms there are in a single hair on your head. He knows your thoughts before you think them.

You know when I sit and when I rise; you perceive my thoughts from afar. You discern my going out and my lying down; you are familiar with all my ways. Before a word is on my tongue you, Lord, know it completely. (Psalm 139:2-4)

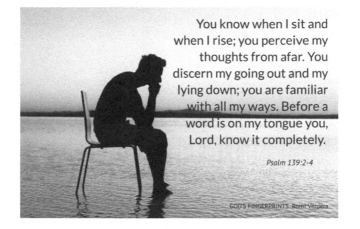

You know when I sit and when I rise; you perceive my thoughts from afar. You discern my going out and my lying down; you are familiar with all my ways. Before a word is on my tongue you, Lord, know it completely.

Psalm 139:2-4

GOD'S FINGERPRINTS Romi Verdera

Chapter Fifteen

THERE IS MORE TO LIFE

I have come that they may have life, and have it to the full. (John 10:10)

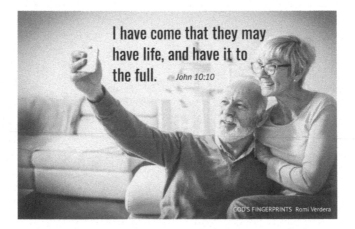

God Touched Me

For many years I thought I was alive. I realized I was just going thru the motion of what seemed to be living; working, sleeping, eating, seeming to have fun, pursuing my material goals in life at the expense of the many other important things in life. It was only when God touched me and I felt his His Spirit that I realized I was dead because He is the tree and I was a deadwood branch separated from Him. I needed to be reborn in the Spirit.

When I was separated from Him, I mean when my conscious life was so filled of just whatever comes my way of experience of this material universe, that was the season of my life I would consider dead to the beautiful life in the spirit. Later, I began enjoying pondering the reality of this spiritual realm revealed to us by Jesus where, in the presence of God, there is freedom, prosperity, joy, hope, love, happiness and peace.

These words are simply expressions of the fullness of life that comes in from finding the life in the spirit. The life in the spirit is the narrow road Jesus is speaking about and the lives being lived only in this material universe is the wide road. It seems to me that we are on this earth to find this narrow road that leads to life. If we do not find it, we simply are mesmerized and weighed down by the common struggle of mankind living just to survive.

Most people live just to survive, keeping the mind sane by enjoying some momentary pleasures in life. We find it in the typical greeting on Mondays, "How is your weekend." Then we come up with explanation of how we found some fun ways to spend the weekend to break the coming week of another grind at the office. Thank God there is a life in the spirit wherein we can live a fulfilled life every single day.

"Again, the kingdom of heaven is like a merchant looking for fine pearls. When he found one of great value, he went away and sold everything he had and bought it. (Matthew 13:45-46)

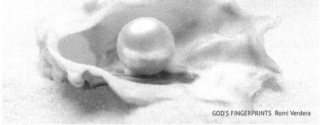

"Again, the kingdom of heaven is like a merchant looking for fine pearls. When he found one of great value, he went away and sold everything he had and bought it." *Matthew 13:45-46*

GOD'S FINGERPRINTS Romi Verdera

My Heart's Response

Dear God, thank you for making me alive. I mean not just breathing alive but enjoying the fullness of life watching Your hand in all creation. I see Your fingerprints everywhere, in the land and mountain, the vastness of the ocean, and the endless blue skies. I see Your love in the smiles of children, friendliness of people, kindness and service of others. The world is teeming with life evolving, manifesting Your grand design. Although there are forces from the will of men and the work of the enemy trying to frustrate the fulfillment of your Your great will, Your power and might prevail, and will bring to completion what You created everything to be. Thank You for making me watch this dance of life of which I am a part of. Amen.

"Heaven and earth will pass away, but my words will never pass away." (Matthew 24:35)

God Is Touching You

You are on this earth to live a full life, not a life of insignificance and mediocrity. You will live a full life only in connection to God. The world's standard of a full life is not God's standard of a full life. Your mind is hypnotized by the things of the world, and many times you think that if you can gain status in this world, you will live a full life. No, that's not it. God's design of the full life is way out different than the world's idea of it. For instance, the world measures a life full by the measure of material wealth one has accumulated.

There is nothing wrong with accumulating wealth as long as you recognize it as God's gift and put it to His service. This whole universe was created by God for us. All wealth belongs to Him. So full life is a life connected to God. And even if you might not have the material wealth you want as much as you want it, you are still living a full life as long as you are living this life in fellowship with Him every day. But even if you have all the wealth that you want, if you are separated from Him, you really have no life.

For what does it profit a man to gain the whole world and forfeit his soul? (Mark 8:36 ESV)

"Otherwise, you may say in your heart, 'My power and the strength of my hand made me this wealth.' "But you shall remember the LORD your God, for it is He who is giving you power to make wealth..." (Deuteronomy 8:17-18)

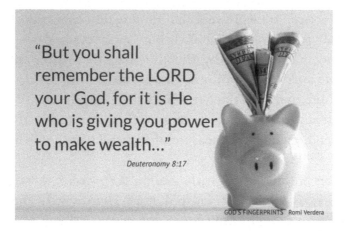

"But you shall remember the LORD your God, for it is He who is giving you power to make wealth..."

Deuteronomy 8:17

GOD'S FINGERPRINTS Romi Verdera

Speak To God In Your Heart

Clear your mind of all thoughts. Your significance lies not in how much seemingly important thoughts there are in your care. Right now, the only important thing is that you are in the presence of God, who gives you everything you have in life. Your life does not consist of things He gave you. Your life is in God, in the deepest part of your being. Your breath is His breath. Your awareness of Him is life. To experience this fullness of life in God, you have to free yourself from the prison of your own self-constructed life in your own mind. Let your mind and heart be free. Let your spirit be free to enjoy the presence of the Spirit of God . Thank God for making you experience your being his child.

For those who are led by the Spirit of God are the children of God.
(Romans 8:14)

Chapter Sixteen

MAY YOUR KINGDOM COME

Our Father in heaven, hallowed be your name, your kingdom come, your will be done, on earth as it is in heaven. (Matthew 6:9-10)

Our Father in heaven, hallowed be your name, your kingdom come, your will be done, on earth as it is in heaven.

Matthew 6:9-10

God Touched Me

I am a recipient of that kingdom. You can too if you have not received it yet. It is not a pie in the sky in the afterlife. It is in the here and now, on this earth in our life. It is God's reign that multiplies bread when I needed it. It calms the storm of our life as Jesus calmed the wind in the sea. It changes water into wine to lighten up our heavy hearts. Yes, wine and not just grape juice. That is for rejoicing and celebrating because He loves making us happy. So do not change the story. It is a kingdom where healing and miracles happen.

"Do not be afraid, little flock, for your Father has been pleased to give you the kingdom." (Luke 12:32)

GOD'S FINGERPRINTS   Romi Verdera

It is a kingdom where He, the King, is generous with forgiveness and mercy. People do not have to continue in guilt and self-condemnation. It is a kingdom where prisoners of poverty are given hope of His providence. It is a kingdom that does not end but lasts forever where citizens do not die. It is a kingdom of peace, joy, hope, and love. I am happy to have been given it, and I want it for everyone; that is why I wrote this book.

———

My Heart's Response

Dear God, thank you for revealing to me Your kingdom here on earth. It is so awesome to think that many ancient kingdoms and nations come and go throughout the centuries, and yet Your kingdom continues to build and spread around the world, and in all continents unrestricted by political boundaries. Your kingdom is built in the mind and heart of people around the globe. It is true the way You said it, to be like a mustard seed that grows into a large tree. I am happy that Your kingdom is within me. I love You God. Amen.

———

God is Touching You

Jesus said that you are in the world, but you do not belong to the world. He is not referring to this material world that God created because everything that God created is good by nature. Jesus was referring to the world system of greed and pride, which is in opposition to God. It is the system of the world, not the world itself. Imagine yourself in the midst of this world. We do not always discern which is of God, and which is against God's system. Many people have been desensitized to the ways of God saying; "everybody in the world does it, so it must be alright." Almost everybody curses today, using the name of God in vain. About four thousand years ago, He got it written about us already in Genesis that we should not use His name in vain. It seems that almost everybody does not seem to care what God said. Cursing is an ancient habit that we human beings could not get rid of from our genes. And we do that with every other perverse action we take. We have made the world system the standard of our living. The more we forget that God is present with us, lovingly watching us live our lives, the more we live in forgetfulness of the fullness of the joyous life lived according to His beautiful plan. You would want to live in His kingdom on this earth in which He rules; wherein He keeps His people away from the devastation of a life lived apart from God. Many live lives in the desperation separated from Him.

"I am the vine; you are the branches. If you remain in me and I in you, you will bear much fruit; apart from me you can do nothing." (John 15:5)

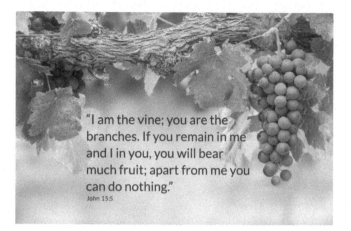

About the people who live connected to God the Scripture says:

"They will be like a tree planted by the water that sends out its roots by the stream. It does not fear when heat comes; its leaves are always green. It has no worries in a year of drought and never fails to bear fruit." (Jeremiah 17:8)

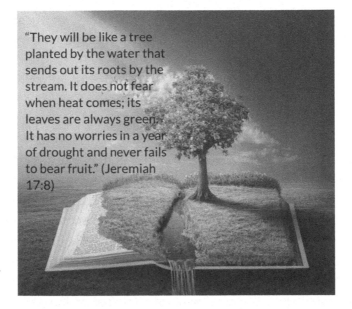

"They will be like a tree planted by the water that sends out its roots by the stream. It does not fear when heat comes; its leaves are always green. It has no worries in a year of drought and never fails to bear fruit." (Jeremiah 17:8)

Speak to God In Your Heart

Be still. Quiet your mind. Ponder those words above which say that God is the vine and you are a branch. The life of the vine is the same life flowing through the branch. Memorize it and keep your mind on it. As it becomes truth in your consciousness, it will make itself real inside of you and in your outward life. The Father is saying to you, "All that I have is yours." In the Gospels, there is a story of the prodigal son who went away, and came back to the father after he lost everything. The father received him back and shared with him everything again.

Do not worry how it will happen that the prosperity of the life of the Father will flow into your life. You are a child of God. It is when people forget this that people live miserably apart from the Father, from whom all things and blessings come. Speak to God your Father. Make sure you spend a lot of time in silence so you could hear what He says. In the beginning, you might think He is not talking back.

Be patient. Be still anyway, even if it seems He is not talking back. I do not know how long you have been trying to spend this kind of prayer in your prayer time. Maybe you never did, or maybe you tried. Maybe perhaps you have heard from Him as I did. I don't know. But I guarantee you this; if you keep practicing being in His presence, He will communicate back to you. You will not question whether He did or did not, because you will know very clearly.

He eagerly wants to dialogue with you. But you have to keep still, and wait. You will have to leave behind all the junks in your mind. I call them junks because compared to the glory of God, all created things are by the apostle Paul's word "rubbish."

God might speak to you in the form of beautiful insights that pop up in your mind. He might come like a "still small voice." He might come like a good memory of the past you did not recognize as Him breaking into your life. He might come in as a split-second flash of vision that will stick with you forever. I don't know how; but I know He will. Be patient. Do not give up. If He does not do it today, He will do it tomorrow, or the next day, or the day after that. He knows the most appropriate time to do it.

Come near to God and he will come near to you. Wash your hands, you sinners, and purify your hearts, you double-minded. (James 4:8)

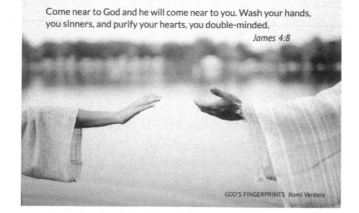

Come near to God and he will come near to you. Wash your hands, you sinners, and purify your hearts, you double-minded.
James 4:8

GOD'S FINGERPRINTS Romi Verdera

Chapter Seventeen

ALL THE THINGS ADDED

But seek first the kingdom of God and his righteousness, and all these things will be added to you. (Matthew 6:33)

But seek first the kingdom of God and his righteousness, and all these things will be added to you. *Matthew 6:33*

GOD'S FINGERPRINTS Romi Verdera

God Touched Me

I can still remember very clearly the exact spot at the dining room where I was in my early 30s when I spoke to God and I told God I do not want to spend the rest of my life on a regular nine-to-five job because I want to spend a lot of time "seeking first the kingdom of heaven."

If, because of my financial need at that time, I end up in a job that would occupy my time working for survival, I would have very little time to pray. My mind would have to be filled with all the earthly things I need to do during my waking hours. I instead wanted to read God's word in the Bible and meditate on them, and make the power of God a reality in my life. I would not be content thinking that they are just written words in a book, or some intellectual ideas in the head. I wanted the power of God in his words inside of me. I wanted to experience and live in the kingdom of God on this earth. God granted me that prayer. I was in my 30s at the time.

I never worked a nine-to-five job since then and I became a self-employed entrepreneur that works at home all my life. I had all the time I can get "seeking the kingdom first." I experienced His word that says, "all these things will be added unto you." The material things I needed were taken cared of too by God. Today my business continues to flourish and becomes a source of provision for me and my family while I do not have to run it directly. I am also able to help out charities, churches, ministries and different projects for the needy. God has blessed me with the time freedom to follow Him.

In the Gospel narrative, Jesus went to Mary and Martha's house. While Martha was stressing herself preparing the food for them to eat, she complained to Jesus that all Mary cared about was sit down and chat with Jesus. Martha asked Jesus to tell Mary to help her prepare their meal. Jesus replied:

"Mary has chosen what is better, and it will not be taken away from her."
(Luke 10:42)

This is what I like about the Bible. The God-inspired authors just tell it the way it is. There is no pretense, no bending of the story to make it appear good. They just present the naked story of the human condition, the craziness of human life. And God presents the alternative ways of living life according to his His will.

———

My Heart's Response

Dear God, It is really true. It was hard to believe at first that you really would add things in to my life if I seek your kingdom first. I was at a very low point in my life when I started paying attention to this verse in the Gospel. I was so broke and all I could think of is work hard, and get myself out of the financial disaster I was in. I tried and tried and I just could not make it out of the deep hole I was in. Then I tried it your way. Sometime in that deep hole I was in, You touched me with your Your words:

> *No branch can bear fruit by itself; it must remain in the vine. Neither can*
> *you bear fruit unless you remain in me. "I am the vine; you are the branches.*
> *If you remain in me and I in you, you will bear much fruit; apart from me*
> *you can do nothing. (John 15:4-5)*

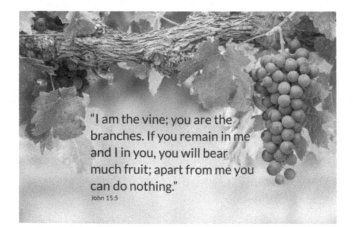

"I am the vine; you are the branches. If you remain in me and I in you, you will bear much fruit; apart from me you can do nothing."
John 15:5

I believed You. Thank you for touching me. Thank you for sometimes putting me in an uncomfortable position so I could pay attention. You have always been so gentle with me, but there were times I needed a jolt. I love You God. Amen.

———

God Is Touching You

You might have been working so hard to make a life. People pay a price for everything. You have to pay a price for enjoying success, and you have to pay a price for suffering failure. Either way, you pay the price. Sometimes you think you are giving your all and yet nothing is coming out of it. There is an alternative. God's way.

God exacts an expensive price for achieving your heart's desire. He wants your all. He does not want you to have anything left on you that you can hold on to in exchange for everything that He will give you. That is because if He gives you everything and you still have some smart on you left, you would think it was your smartness that got you what you received from Him. God wants you to be so sure that you acknowledge that it was Him who worked in your life, and fulfilled His promise that "all these things will be added unto you."

You are reading this book because He is clarifying this thing to you. When you spend much time in the meditation of the truth of God's ways, do not think of it as wasting time. Do not think that you should instead work more and harder because it is work that produces results that will improve your life. It is true that it is indeed work that produces result,. But you can only work so much. The amount of work you can do is limited. But the amount of result God can add to what you have done is unlimited. So remember, without God touching the work you do, you are limited to the result of your own effort and it could amount to nothing even. Ponder on this.

Unless the Lord builds the house those who build it labor in vain. (Psalm 127:1)

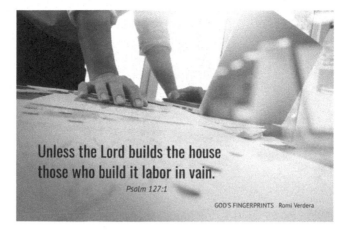

Unless the Lord builds the house
those who build it labor in vain.
Psalm 127:1

GOD'S FINGERPRINTS Romi Verdera

Speak to God in Your Heart

Be still. Be aware of your breathing. Sense the air going in and out of your lungs. Every bit of it is God's supply of energy to every cell in your body. You did not do anything to deserve it. Every ounce of air entering your lungs is filled with energy transported by your lungs to your bloodstream that supplies the energy to your bones and muscles and brain. You could not even read or think if it were not for God supplying you with His breath.

Be aware that this energy supply is just a sample of the rest of what God is providing you in different forms. It could be health, relationship, money, intelligence, wisdom, faith, hope, love, everything. God is the source of all of them. Thank God and keep silent. Just be aware that He is there around you, inside you, above you, underneath you, and in the whole universe. He longs to break into your experience.

But they that wait upon the Lord shall renew their strength; they shall mount up with wings as eagles. (Isaiah 40:31 KJV)

But they that wait upon the Lord shall renew their strength; they shall mount up with wings as eagles.

Isaiah 40:31 KJV

Chapter Eighteen

AFFLICTIONS IN LIFE

"The righteous person may have many troubles but the Lord delivers him from them all..." (Psalm 34:19)

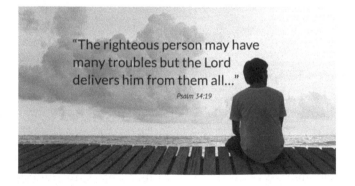

God Touched Me

How do you feel when you read this Scripture?. Do you feel like, "I've heard that before. How come He does not take away many of my afflictions?" I want to help you make it happen for you. I mean, let your afflictions go away. Start spending a few minutes a day, making the word of God real in your life. How do you do it? Read it again, and again. Meditate on it until you feel in your mind, heart and soul that you are believing it. Cancel any reason, justification, doubt and contrary belief that others have implanted in your mind. You came to believe them as to why you deserve your afflictions, and they will not go away. You will have to consciously let them go.

Ask God to give you the "grace of faith." Faith is not just an intellectual agreement to what was said. Your intellect may say yes, I believe it, but deep in your "heart," you really don not. You will have to keep on thinking about it until your heart agrees. Then you have a "spirit" in the deepest part of you. It is the one that connects to God. It is there where God dwells. It is not the same as your intellect and heart. When your spirit becomes led by God, your spirit then leads your heart and mind. When that happens, the "Scripture" comes alive in your life and the word of God becomes real inside of you. God really becomes your God; not just an occasional idea in your head.

For those who are led by the Spirit of God are the children of God. (Romans 8:14)

My Heart's Response

Dear God, thank you for the life that I have enjoyed all these years. They were initially not all pleasant in the beginning, but those unpleasantness trained me in strengthening my resolve to cast away all the obstacles. They strengthened my faith that You would help me pass through the tumultuous times. They showed me very clearly that You were there fighting my battles for me. There is no victory without a fight, no resurrection without death.

You made me learn the hard way. But it was all worth it. You made all your promises in your word real in my life. For all your help, guidance and consolation, I am very grateful. You showed me that there is nothing more beautiful and meaningful than a life lived in fellowship with You. I love you God. Amen.

God Is Touching You

You continue to read this book because you continue to thirst for God. Behind this thirst is the dissatisfaction you have for many things. I do not know what you are dissatisfied with. I know for most people, it's either lack of money, or relationship, or job situation, or health, or you may be rich but bored and is missing something that you can not point a finger on. Our affliction is a result of our separation from the ultimate good that God is. It is not that we are separated from our good; it is just that we can not find our connection to it. Jesus showed us the way. It is His constant contact with the Father that enables him to feed the five thousand, heal the sick, change water into wine, and gather the fish on the water for Peter.

One of those days Jesus went out to a mountainside to pray, and spent the night praying to God. (Luke 6:12)

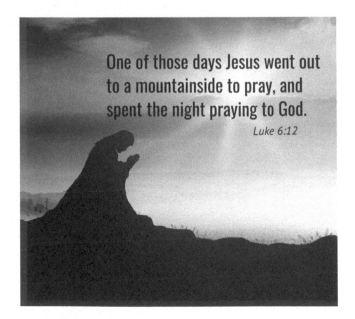

One of those days Jesus went out to a mountainside to pray, and spent the night praying to God.
Luke 6:12

There was nothing He cannot do. And that was because of His prayer life. God is touching you today. He wants you to learn to pray like Jesus. Ponder on this.

———

Speak to God In Your Heart

How could Jesus been praying all night? He knew the Father knew everything He was going to ask. He said that to us. This is where we miss all the time. Most of us pray and just keep saying our petition, hoping God heard and maybe He will change His mind about giving us what we are asking for. We bargain telling God our promises of things we will do in exchange for His favor. And after we say them all, we stop praying and leave Him without waiting to hear what He have to say.

We do not give Him time to express His love for us. So we leave the pews in the church, or our room of prayer, or wherever we are on the road hoping God heard us. God is touching your heart asking you to be still. Empty your mind and heart and just be still and wait for Him. Practice trusting. You might say "but how can I trust Him when I have no experience to stand on, where I can say that He saved me out of my trouble." Be still. Quiet your mind and rest on Him. Get a scripture and meditate on it like,

"Can a mother forget the baby at her breast and have no compassion on the child she has borne? Though she may forget, I will not forget you!" (Isaiah 49:15)

"Can a mother forget the baby at her breast and have no compassion on the child she has borne? Though she may forget, I will not forget you!"
Isaiah 49:15)

As you meditate on the Scripture, it becomes real in your experience. You might not perceive how it would be real. But like a seed that turns into a tiny shoot, then little buds appear, then leaves, then flowers. The fruit of your meditation and prayer will manifest later in ways you could not even conceive of as resulting from your meditations. It may be a person that will show up in your life, a job offer, an extraordinary opportunity you might not even be expecting. It might manifest first in just a glimpse of insight, or hope. Later, it will manifest in some concrete reality. Be still. Meditate. Pray.

———

Chapter Nineteen

ISRAEL'S LOVE STORY

I am my beloved's and my beloved is mine. (Song of Solomon 6:3)

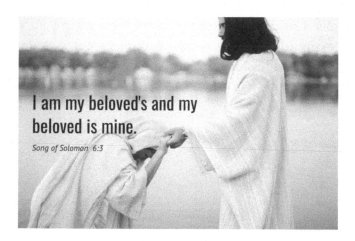

God Touched Me

I asked my mother when I was young why she named me Romeo. That is my real name. And she told me that it was because she watched the movie "Romeo and Juliet," so she named me Romeo. I did not see the movie myself until I became an adult. All

I knew was that it was a love story. As I grew older, I adapted my nickname "Romi." When people ask me for my name today, I say my name is "Romi." It prevents me from being asked, "where is Juliet?"

I believe I was in high school when I thought I want to think of my name as Israel. And that was because as I read the Bible, I start to see parallels of my own life with the life of the tribe of Israel. God is the lover and Israel is His beloved, and Israel kept on turning away from Him.

I was beginning to see the story of the Israelites' story as the love story between God and His people Israel. Israel has a long history of running away from God, and God is always devising all kinds of ways to get them back to Himself. Now that I am old, I look back and the more I see how real my life story being parallel to Israel's story. The good thing is that the Bible has a good ending. Jesus finally comes back for his spotless bride, having reconciled humankind to God. And I am a part of that love story.

"And I, when I am lifted up from the earth, will draw all people to myself." (*John 12:32*)

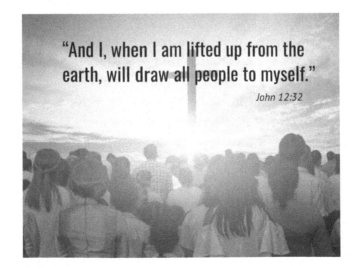

My Heart's Response

Dear God, I am so awed at how You maneuver all events of history to fulfill your plans. I am so awed at your persistent unwavering unconditional love for humankind. Thank you for opening up my eyes to this reality. This is the meaning of life. This is the truth that human intellect is searching for and without the awareness of this reality, the human intellect is bankrupt. The intellect feeds on a whole lot of worldly empty seeming realities. The timeline of the history of humankind is the narrative of your love story, You being the lover and humankind being the beloved. I see my place in this love story. I am a recipient of your overwhelming love. It is breathtaking being caught in this divine love story. Thank you God. Amen.

———

God is Touching You.

I encourage you to meditate on the fact that the reason why God created you is to share His love with you. It is Him who is the source of love, and the source of our life's meaning. You are a character in this divine love story. When you discover the depth and reality of God's love for you, your heart will have no other choice but to love God back. You do not have to be obliged to love God. Loving God back is a natural reaction of a heart that feels loved. It is not something that is imposed. Love is freely given. Look back into your life and find instances that you perceive is God's act of loving you. It actually is everything that you are experiencing even now. But take time to consciously be aware of them.

"Can a mother forget the baby at her breast and have no compassion on the child she has borne? Though she may forget, I will not forget you!" (Isaiah 49:15)

> "Can a mother forget the baby at her breast and have no compassion on the child she has borne? Though she may forget, I will not forget you!"
>
> *Isaiah 49:15*

Speak To God In Your Heart

Be still. Quiet your mind. Dwell in the awareness that we are in the presence of God who loves us. Love is something we do not learn by thinking. It is the function of the heart. It is a soul thing. Ask God to let you feel His love, then keep still in silence. The heart has reasons that not even reason can grasp. Even in life, we sometimes ask how can this person love this other person?. We are unable to enter the heart experience of another person when it comes to love.

We will only understand love when God pours his love on us. I can not cannot bring you to the experience of God's love. I can only show you the way. The first thing I do when when I wake up in the morning is kiss the crucifix with love and say good morning to Jesus. I could feel the love. I never used to feel that. I don't know when this feeling of love started happening. I kiss the feet of Jesus on the crucifix too before I sleep. I used to pray dry prayers but not anymore. I know God put that love in my heart one day which I can't remember when. Your journey to the heart of God is your own journey. You can start by thanking Him for everything you can thank Him for. Then be still, knowing He is right there with you, listening and loving you. Just bask yourself in his loving look.

I will give thanks to you, Lord, with all my heart; I will tell of all your wonderful deeds. (Psalm 9:1)

———

Chapter Twenty

EVERYDAY IS CHRISTMAS

The Word became flesh and made his dwelling among us. (John 1:14)

God Touched Me

Christmas to me was just an event that happened 2000 years ago in some remote village on a dark night, until I realize that I was born into this world to be another Jesus on this earth. And so are you, and everyone else. We were just not aware of it. It is a reality we were born to discover. When I came to the realization that

Christmas was not a onetime happening, but Christ Himself being born in me, and living His life in me day by day. He is loving people, building the kingdom of God. Then I realize I was not just an observer of a past event, but a participant in the life of the living Jesus today. Hence, everyday is Christmas. God touched ground on this earth that first Christmas night. He came for us all.

"The Spirit of the Lord is on me, because he has anointed me to proclaim good news to the poor. He has sent me to proclaim freedom for the prisoners and recovery of sight for the blind, to set the oppressed free." (Luke 4:18)

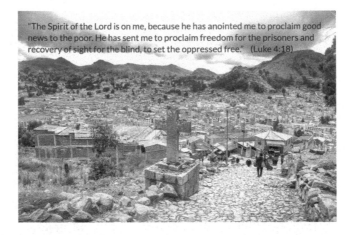

The reason for His coming to this earth is the same reason for our being born here. God is giving birth to his His life on this earth day by day. He is building his kingdom in the hearts and minds of people. First, there were twelve, then there were 72 that He sent out to preach and heal, then there were 3000 that God touched by His Holy Spirit at Pentecost, and today there are 2 billion Christians around the world. God is birthing Jesus in all nations.

———

My Heart's Response
Dear God, thank You for revealing Yourself to me. Discovering

You opened up to me a whole new world, a life in the spirit. It is almost like discovering a parallel universe where one can see You and live in your Your presence. And in Your presence, all negativity melts. I never knew love until you put it in my heart. Or maybe love was there all along but it just could not escape because my heart was hardened. I may not understand all the things You do, but I am just happy my heart knows that I am loved beyond understanding, and that you gave me the capacity to love you back. I am just joyful and thankful for everything.

> *The kingdom of heaven is like treasure hidden in a field. When a man found it, he hid it again, and then in his joy went and sold all he had and bought that field.* (Matthew 13:44)

———

God Is Touching You

I hope and pray that you are seeing your place in God's grand design of creation. He knew you before the foundation of the world. He formed you in your mother's womb. He has a plan for you and it is good. In the beginning, you might think that you are just an accident. Or maybe you already have a glimpse that you really were created for a purpose, and yet you could not figure out how to fulfill your destiny.

It is a song in your heart that you know it is there, but don't know how to sing it. Take your time. Meditate on these thoughts. Ask God for revelation. That is how He reveals himself, a little at a time. Just as you do not notice how a seed grows into a little shoot, into a shrub, then into a tree with you noticing every day that it is growing, so is the knowledge of His will in your life. He reveals it little by little.

> *He told them another parable: "The kingdom of heaven is like a mustard seed, which a man took and planted in his field. Though it is the smallest of all seeds, yet when it grows, it is the largest of garden plants and becomes*

a tree, so that the birds come and perch in its branches." (Matthew 13:31-32)

———

Speak To God In Your Heart

As you meditate on how God the Father is continually giving birth to Jesus into the heart of people, invite Jesus to be born in your heart and mind. He is already there or you would not have reached to this page in the book. You just have to be conscious of that reality. Speak to Him and welcome Him into your heart. Express to Him your desire to fellowship with Him. Today is Christmas in your heart. Celebrate today. Be still and make your mind dwell in the reality that Jesus wants to be born and grow in your mind and heart.

I no longer live, but Christ lives in me. The life I now live in the body, I live by faith in the Son of God, who loved me and gave himself for me. (Galatians 2:20)

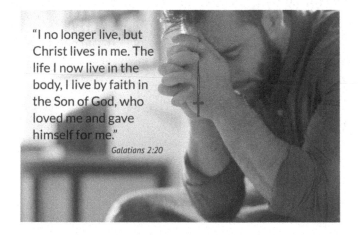

"I no longer live, but Christ lives in me. The life I now live in the body, I live by faith in the Son of God, who loved me and gave himself for me."
Galatians 2:20

———

Chapter Twenty-One

GAME OF CHESS WITH GOD

Where were you when I laid the earth's foundation? Tell me, if you understand. (Job 38:4)

Where were you when I laid the earth's foundation? Tell me, if you understand.

Job 8:4

God Touched Me

I look at my life like a game of chess in which God and I are playing. I have to constantly figure out what He is thinking. He let me play the game and I enjoy it. Sometimes He attacks and takes over my pieces, and I lose my plan of advance. I try and struggle to win. I get blocked, cornered, sometimes get to advance and have some winning moves. Finally, His Son the King dies and I win, not because I am smart but because He let me win, as a gift to my being human, by grace.

Later, I find that His fingerprints are on my chess pieces too. He let me move them with my own hands while His Spirit is on my breath. So it is God who wins and I just enjoy the game and share the victory.

"For in him we live and move and have our being." (Acts 17:28)

———

My Heart's Response

Dear God, I can't even move my finger without you letting me. I owe You every bit of wits I have and every ounce of energy in my body. Although I make up plans for my life because You gave me mind, imagination, and free will to make them, it is You who inspire me to come up with good and right ideas for the good of my life. I thank You God for always guiding me. I love You God. Amen.

Whether you turn to the right or to the left, your ears will hear a voice behind you, saying, "This is the way; walk in it." (Isaiah 30:21)

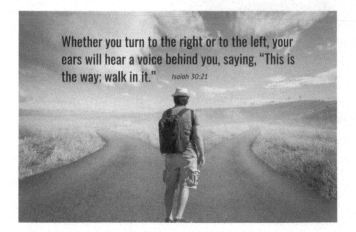

God Is Touching You

Sometimes people say that life is like a game. They call it "the game of life." And you bet your life in it. In a game, some win and others lose. God wants to play this game of life with you. But God's game of life is a win-win proposition. He sets the rules and if you play by the rules you are guaranteed to win. And even if it seems like you're losing in life, you still win. And if you missed playing by the rules because you missed knowing it, He lets His Son save you the misery of losing and allows you to win. You betted your life and you lose and you're supposed to have no life anymore because you lost the game. But the Son paid for your lost life and He gives you His own. And all you have to do is accept it. Be still and meditate on this for some moments until it sinks into you.

You were bought at a price; do not become slaves of human beings. (1 Corinthians 7:23)

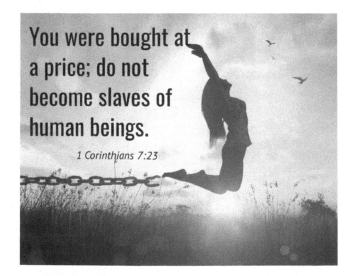

Speak To God In Your Heart

You might think that you are just one of the over seven billion people on planet earth, so why would God even pay attention to you, much less love you specially. But He does love you. He knows the aches of your heart and your joys. He knows your desires and frustrations. He knows your dream and the hope you have given up. He knows your delight and your brokenness. He created you and knows your possibilities. He wants you to play this game of life with Him. He designed you to win and not to lose and fail. So gather the game pieces of your life and play with Him. He will make you win. He wants you to win. Thank God for the opportunity He is giving you. Be still and meditate on this. Talk to Him. Pray.

For the mountains may depart and the hills be removed, but my steadfast love shall not depart from you, and my covenant of peace shall not be removed," says the Lord, who has compassion on you. (Isaiah 54:10)

Chapter Twenty-Two

HEAVEN AND HELL

Answer me quickly, Lord; my spirit fails. Do not hide your face from me or I will be like those who go down to the pit. (Psalm 143:7)

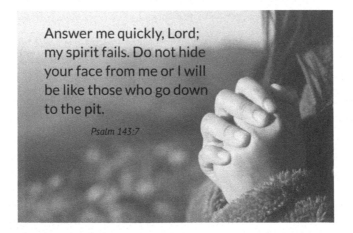

Answer me quickly, Lord; my spirit fails. Do not hide your face from me or I will be like those who go down to the pit.

Psalm 143:7

God Touched Me

A few seconds in hell; that is how I would call this experience that I had once when I was in my 30s. As I sat on the beach looking up at the clouds and I thought, "What if there is no heaven, there is no God, and I am just imagining all this heavenly stuffs?" It was such a beautiful day and all of a sudden it seems the whole universe turned so cold on me, meaningless, sad, empty, a sort of state of a void so deep inside my soul, a feeling of fear and dread of the noth-ingness of life. Those are probably moments when if extended long enough, a person just wants to disappear from this earth and end one's life. It was a hell of a moment, a real dreadful hellish moment. I would say it is an experience of being separated from God for a brief moment. I thank God that He snapped me out of it right away and I am back to the real colorful world where God dwells and His presence permeates every atom of the universe and his Holy Spirit dwelling in me. I believe God just showed me for a brief moment what it is to be in hell and separated from him. I would not want that kind of moment ever again. That was enough few seconds of experience for me to understand hell.

In contrast, God's visitations in my soul throughout my life are many and I wish He does it every day but He does not. Most of the time I just wake up in the morning and say "Where are you, God? You did not speak to me last night when I was asleep. I did not see you in my dreams. Don't be so far, please." Then I would pray, read the Bible, and simply sense that He is there even if I don't see Him. He is near. He is in my breath. I believe one moment of visitation in which one encounters God is enough for one to know the reality of heaven, God, the spiritual realm. I experienced very few of them so ecstatic I could understand why David said:

"Better is one day in your court than a thousand elsewhere..." (Psalm 84:10)

It made me understand how biblical people like Moses, Abra-ham, Jacob, David and many prophets became who they are because God really visited them. Now, Jesus, He is the ultimate deal. He only spoke and did what He heard and saw from the Father which meant He experienced God every moment.

"I am telling you what I have seen in the Father's presence..." (John 8:38)

Because of the narrative in the Bible, we think that those bible heroes were always in the presence of God and they were always high in ecstatic experience. No, they were not. Those encounters with God were few compared to the daily routine of just living a life longing for God's closer manifestation. Most of their days were lived in faith in the God who sometimes showed up but most of the time He was the God behind the scene. That is how God designed our lives to be; a life lived in faith.

They are these moments of heaven that anchor our faith in the reality of God's love and heaven, when we are tempted to despair. Jesus said,

"However, do not rejoice that the spirits submit to you, but rejoice that your names are written in heaven." (Luke 10:20)

"... rejoice that your names are written in heaven." (Luke 10:20)

Most of our days would be spent on the daily grind of doing our daily routine. Without faith in the fact that God loves us and that "our names are written in heaven," and that we are doing it all for His glory, we will miss the "rejoicing" part in the normal course of our life.

My Heart's Response

Dear God, I thank you for these momentary encounters with You that enable me to know You by experience. Without these, I would feel so far away from You. And when sometimes you seem distant, I pray that You strengthen my faith to know that you are still with me. Let me always be reminded that as You said, I should rejoice that my name is written in heaven. Thank You for Your love. I love You God. Amen.

How priceless is your unfailing love, O God! (Psalm 36:7)

————

God Is Touching You

What father hides himself from his child when his child wants to be with him? God longs to be with you. He wants you to desire His friendship. All of us are God's children. He created us all so He can share His life with us. In human families, not all sons are friendly to their fathers. Some sons are friends to their peers but not friends to their fathers. Some are closer to their friends but are strangers to their own fathers. It is not always the fault of the sons because unfortunately, some fathers provoke their sons to be so.

Fathers, do not provoke your children to anger, but bring them up in the discipline and instruction of the Lord. (Ephesians 6:4 ESV)

God is way not like human fathers. God our Father wants you to be His friend. Majority of times, love of a human father is conditional. God our Father loves us unconditionally. He wants to be close to you. He wants to commune with you in your prayers. He wants to fellowship with you in your quiet moments. Jesus showed us the love of God in the parable of the prodigal son. It is an unconditional love independent of whatever we might have done. Meditate on it until you feel the love of God in your heart.

"'My son,' the father said, 'you are always with me, and everything I have is yours." (Luke 15:31)

Speak To God In Your Heart

Find a quiet place and be still. Give all your concerns, hesitations, anxieties, reluctance to God. He wants them all. He does not want anything between you and Him. Speak to Him. Express to Him how you miss paying as much attention to Him as you should have. Ask His forgiveness for ignoring His invitations in your heart. There were many times in your life you felt you were really not as close to Him as you should have been. And yet you tried to avoid the encounter thinking that He might ask you of things you might not be able to give. Believe that if He does, it is just because He wants to give you a whole lot better than the one you are holding onto. You might not be ready to give Him your all. That is alright. He is not rushing you. But He just wants you to be near Him. He loves you just the same. There is nothing you can do that can separate you from His love for you.

And I am convinced that nothing can ever separate us from God's love. Neither death nor life, neither angels nor demons, neither our fears for today nor our worries about tomorrow—not even the powers of hell can separate us from God's love. (Romans 8:38)

Nothing can ever separate us from God's love. Neither death nor life, neither angels nor demons, neither our fears for today nor our worries about tomorrow—not even the powers of hell can separate us from God's love.

Romans 8:38

Speak to God. Thank Him for His love. Be still and stay longer in His presence. You do not have to think of anything. Just be like a child sitting side by side with his father who is his friend by the shore watching the horizon, the clouds in the sky. No words, no thoughts, just beautifully enjoying the moment together.

Chapter Twenty-Three

SEARCHING FOR HIS FINGERPRINTS

Speak, Lord, for your servant is listening. (1 Samuel 3:9)

Speak, Lord,
for your
servant is
listening.

1 Samuel 3:9

God Touched Me

When I look back in my life, I see various levels of intensity in my God experiences. As I was growing up, I always have this sense that there is more to desire than the way I pray, the way I relate to

God, the way I think about Him and the way I live my life as a person created by Him. When I was younger I somehow knew vaguely my reason for living. Life circumstance changes, and what I sometimes think the right direction of my life, apparently becomes not as I thought of it. As I grew older, the necessity of coming to God for guidance becomes clearer and clearer. Sometimes the change in direction is so huge that I wonder how I could have been so wrong. Now, I think maybe God had to let me go through those detours, because there were things I had to learn from those out of the way path. Today, I am convinced that it is how God really works. I sometimes ended up in the wrong direction to lead me to the right way. The more it happens, the more I search for the light of His way. One day I can see His fingerprints and the next day I feel like I am on my own. And God does that to make me keep searching for Him always.

"For my thoughts are not your thoughts, neither are your ways my ways," declares the Lord. "As the heavens are higher than the earth, so are my ways higher than your ways and my thoughts than your thoughts." (Isaiah 55:8-9)

———

My Heart's Response

Dear God, I thank you for the times You fill me with the feeling of Your nearness. I thank You too for the times I feel You are quiet and seem so far. Those times, my mind knows You are near just the same, although I can not feel You. I now know that is Your way of making my heart long for You. Let me have a fresh communion with You every day. Thank you, God. I love You. Amen.

———

God Is Touching You

You must have found some of God's fingerprints that is why you are reading this book. What I mean is that you are God-connected already. Otherwise, you would not even care to find more of His fingerprints. He reveals Himself in different ways and leaves fingerprints along the way. Then I realized, His hand is not just on my life but in everyone's life. His hand is in the history of the world, in ancient events, in the happenings at this present time, and the future is unfolding with His hands on it. His fingerprint is on every tick of the clock.

> *"All the days ordained for me were written in your book before one of them came to be."* (Psalm 139:16)

You must have known His reality, felt His presence, heard His voice, and grasped His words. And you want more of it that is why you are reading this book. Like a traveler searching the right path, you are looking to the trail others have traveled to get to the presence of God. You want to see the footprints of others in following the path with God's fingerprints. I can only show you the path He led me to. You will have to walk into God's presence yourself.

> *But when you pray, go into your room, close the door and pray to your Father, who is unseen. Then your Father, who sees what is done in secret, will reward you. (Matthew 6:6)*

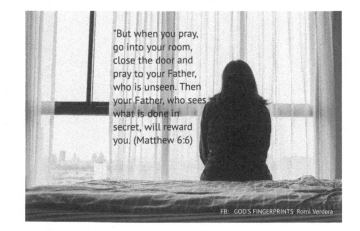

———

Speak To God In Your Heart

Be still. Forget about your cares. Care only for one thing, to be in God's presence. Sense your breathing in and breathing out and be grateful for every breath God has given you from the time you came out of your mother's womb to the present. He will give you more because He wants to reveal Himself more to you. Thank Him and express your gratefulness and love.

He breathed on them and said, "Receive the Holy Spirit." (John 20:22)

He breathed on them and said, "Receive the Holy Spirit." (John 20:22)

———

Chapter Twenty-Four

HUNGER FOR GOD

You, God, are my God, earnestly I seek you; I thirst for you, my whole being longs for you..." (Psalm 63:1)

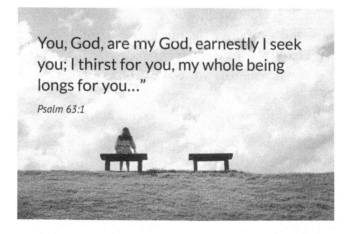

God Touched Me

The bible is boring for someone who never encountered the God of the Bible personally. It is not an academic workbook for intellectual life consumption. It is the word of God for spiritual life nourishment for those who are thirsty for Him. It is spiritual food for the spiritually hungry, not intellectual information for the curious. To treat it as just intellectual information makes it dry, and most of it even illogical from human standpoint. Once one encounters God in experience, God's word becomes alive. I don't expect many people to understand what I just said. It is a kind of knowing where I know I am in God's presence, and He is there face to face with me even though I do not see His face with my eyes. It is not just a thought. Every part of my body feels His presence. Every atom of my being is energized by His presence. It's like electric peace and love. I don't think we will have a full understanding of why some encounter God and others don not. God is sovereign and we can only desire and pray that He gives us one. He gave me one when I was 33 years old. After that, He keeps on giving one every now and then. But after that initial visitation of His presence, the knowledge of His presence stays with me every single moment of every day. I miss it when I don't sense it. I always want to go back to it. Why me? I don't know. I was just as bad or worse than a lot people at my age then. That encounter was the same encounter the disciples had at Pentecost. I get excited even now when I see pictures of Pentecost. I feel like blurting out and saying: "That's it. That's what He did for me." That encounter did it for me. You can feed me to the lion and I won't deny that Jesus, God, the Holy Spirit, and heaven is real. And that is why I am excited about God every day. I pray that you long for that encounter too and that He gives it to you.

As the deer longs for streams of water, so I long for you, O God. (Psalm 42:1)

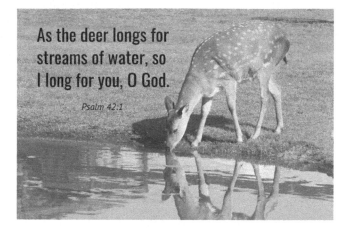

As the deer longs for streams of water, so I long for you, O God.

Psalm 42:1

—————

My Heart's Response

Dear God, after I felt your intense touch, I started having a deeper understanding of Your words. Thank You for filling me with your Holy Spirit. My life has never been the same since then. When I read the Bible, I feel like I am part of the story. When I read the words of Jesus, I feel the words He was speaking were being spoken to me. When I read the stories of Abraham, Joseph, Moses, David, and the apostles, I could feel the same spirit in them in me. Thank You God. I love You God. Amen.

"In the last days,' God says,' I will pour out my Spirit on all people. Your sons and daughters will prophesy, your young men will see visions, your old men will dream dreams."' (Acts 2:17)

—————

God Is Touching You

Believe that there is so much more to the experience of knowing and being known by God. There is so much more to your experience of loving and being loved by God. You might feel that loving God with all your mind, heart and soul does not characterize your relationship with Him. Well, now that you know there is more, there is really nothing you can do to attain this more and deeper experience but to ask for His grace to allow you to taste more of it and wait, and expect. Be still. Take your time and spend quiet times with God in the silence of your heart. You might want to read the scripture but as you come across a phrase that touches you, stop. Close the book and dwell on it."

"Be still before the Lord and wait patiently for him." (Psalm 37:7)

Speak To God In Your Heart

Learn how to speak to God using His own words in the Scripture. For instance, repeat in your mind and heart this Bible phrase:

"Search me, God, and know my heart; test me and know my anxious thoughts. See if there is any offensive way in me, and lead me in the way everlasting." (Psalm 139:23-24)

Repeat it as many times as you can slowly. You may even take a break in between just to be able to feel the meaning of the phrase. Keep repeating it until you mean it. You are not repeating it so God may hear you. He heard you the first time. He heard you even before you say it in your mind and heart. You are repeating it for your own self so that your heart will align with your mind. Your mind and heart will align with your spirit where God dwells. When your spirit then leads your mind and heart, you are near the presence of God. It is not that God is far. It is that your mind and heart might be far from God. But God is near all the time. Be still. Speak to Him. Take your time. Stay as long as you can.

———

Chapter Twenty-Five

DRUNK DISCIPLES

These people are not drunk, as you suppose. It's only nine in the morning! No, this is what was spoken by the prophet Joel: "In the last days, God says, I will pour out my Spirit on all people. Your sons and daughters will prophesy, your young men will see visions, your old men will dream dreams. (Acts 2:15-17)

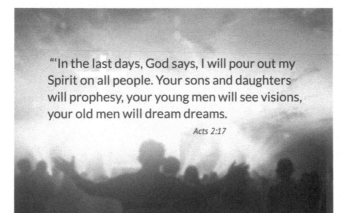

"'In the last days, God says, I will pour out my Spirit on all people. Your sons and daughters will prophesy, your young men will see visions, your old men will dream dreams.

Acts 2:17

God Touched Me

Drunk is drunk anywhere you go. A drunk Jew, a drunk Filipino, a drunk Latino, a drunk American, a drunk European all look, walk, and talk the same. In the Book of Acts, when the Holy Spirit came down to the apostles at Pentecost, they looked like they were drunk. This is so clear in the Bible. We just have become so sophisticated that we invent a picture of a spiritual person close to God as appropriately clasping both hands in prayer silently looking down with eyes closed. It is as if that is the only way to properly encounter God. Drunk also translates as intoxicated, feeling-high, and ecstatic, beyond oneself. These are terms we mostly associate with drinking alcohol or getting high on drugs, so we don not talk about this manifestation in spirituality. The Bible says things as it is as God does things to people. That is why for so long I kept silent about these experiences of encounters with God in my dreams, in my imagination, in my prayers, for fear of being ridiculed or misunderstood. But I kept them in my journals. In the New York flood during the Sandy Hurricane, I lost several of my journals. Our basement was flooded. When I woke up on my 65th birthday thinking of writing "God's Fingerprints," I looked them up around my house, on my bookshelves, and on some plastic crates in the basement and I found some of them again. So in this book, I would pick out some from those journals and some of what I can recall and share them with you here. I know people would say, "What is he saying? Is he drunk or maybe high?" We often hear of "filled with the Holy Spirit." It is hard to explain but that's what it is.

My Heart's Response

Dear God, I thank you for your touches. If you did not touch my soul I would feel so far from You. How is it that You care for me when You have the whole universe? Last night I felt Your love penetrating my soul and I cannot help but sob. It's been a long time since I last felt that. Thank You for Your surprise touches that leave Your fingerprints in my soul. I wish they were more often. I love You, God. Amen.

"Praise the Lord, my soul; all my inmost being, praise his holy name."
(Psalm 103:1)

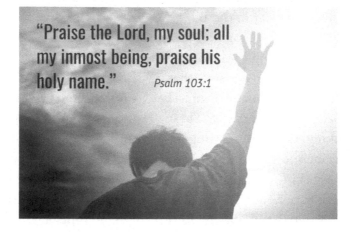

God Is Touching You

God wants to touch you if you will let Him. He wants to fill you with His Holy Spirit, the same Spirit that was in Jesus when He walked on this earth and performed all His miracles. It is the same Holy Spirit that raised Him from the dead. It is the same Holy Spirit that Jesus gave to His disciples at Pentecost. You only have to open yourself and surrender everything to Him. Your life will change and you will be at peace and joyful. Your life will have a new meaning you never perceived before. Be still. Talk to God. He is your Father. Talk to Jesus. He sends the Holy Spirit to us. Take your time. Keep still. Dwell on this truth in your consciousness.

"But the Advocate, the Holy Spirit, whom the Father will send in my name, will teach you all things and will remind you of everything I have said to you." (John 14:26)

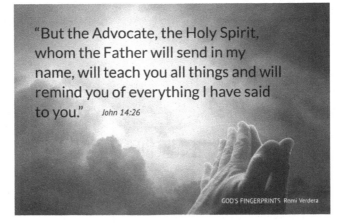

"But the Advocate, the Holy Spirit, whom the Father will send in my name, will teach you all things and will remind you of everything I have said to you." *John 14:26*

GOD'S FINGERPRINTS Romi Verdera

Speak To God In Your Heart

Speaking to God is not just you speaking. You should allow a lot of time for listening. Your mind does not want that. Your mind just wants to keep on thinking. It cannot stand the silence. Remember, your mind is not you. You own it. It is like your computer. It is a tool. If you do not know how to direct it, it will direct you. That is why it is sometimes said, "you are your worst enemy." So, practice calming your mind. Focus for a few moments on your breathing. Just be aware of the air coming in and out of your nostrils and lungs. When your mind is focused on this, it stops thinking. When it stops thinking, then think of God and speak to God. Just speak to Him as a friend speaks to a friend, as a child speaks to his father. Always keep much time for just being still and being quiet waiting for God to utter something inside you. It might be an inspiration, consolation, a sensation, a feeling of joy. He comes in different ways.

Call to me and I will answer you, and will tell you great and hidden things that you have not known. (Jeremiah 33:3 ESV)

Chapter Twenty-Six

CHILD OF GOD

"Truly I tell you, unless you change and become like little children, you will never enter the kingdom of heaven." (Matthew 18:3)

God Touched Me

I am a child of God first before any other thing. Then next is that I am a father, husband, friend, businessman, writer, leader and many other roles. Being a child of God enables me to enter the kingdom of heaven even on this earth. Many people think that the kingdom of heaven is up in the sky. It is there and it is here too. It is a life of peace, joy and love as a child of God. One may fail as a spouse, parent, businessman, or any other role but that is not as bad as one who fails as knowing his identity as a child of God. Being a child of God is my REAL IDENTITY. All the other roles are just wrapping paper identities that I might succeed or fail in wrapping myself with. But if I forget my identity of being a loved child of my Father God, then I really lose everything. For as long as I know my identity as a child of God, I have a chance of being restored, being healed, and go on living in peace, joy and love.

———

My Heart's Response

Dear God, there was a time in my life when I was younger that I was proud and arrogant of my capabilities. I thought I could succeed in life just by my own efforts and smartness. After everything I tried just became a collection of my own failures, I came to You for help. Like a little child coming to his father because he keeps falling and cannot stand, you picked me up and taught me that I cannot do anything apart from you. That was a hard lesson to learn. I learned it the hard way. I thank you for that lesson, and I thank you that I learned it early in life. I love You God. Amen.

I am the vine; you are the branches. Whoever abides in me and I in him, he it is that bears much fruit, for apart from me you can do nothing. (John 15:5)

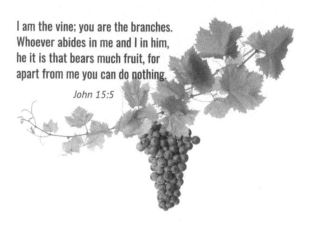

I am the vine; you are the branches.
Whoever abides in me and I in him,
he it is that bears much fruit, for
apart from me you can do nothing.

John 15:5

God Is Touching You

God wants to strip you of all that is not of Him. Whatever is
not of Him is an unnecessary heavy baggage that you carry. He
wants you to be free. He wants you to live a full life.

> *"'Come to me, all who labor and are heavy laden, and I will give you rest.
> Take my yoke upon you, and learn from me, for I am gentle and lowly in
> heart, and you will find rest for your souls. For my yoke is easy, and my
> burden is light'" (Matt 11:28-30 ESV)*

He loves you and knows what is best for you. You are a child of
God and as a good Father who is all-knowing and all love, he cannot
desire anything less than what is best for you. He knows you more
than you know yourself. Allow Him to transform you with His
spirit according to His beautiful design. Surrender is a hard thing to
do because pride is a hard thing to let go of. The more you trust in
His love, the easier it gets to just rest in God and be at peace with
His will. When your will aligns with His will, as you enjoy being
united with Him, all that is not of Him melts away. Peace, joy and
love become the atmosphere of your soul.

But the fruit of the Spirit is love, joy, peace, patience, kindness, goodness, faithfulness, gentleness, self-control; against such things there is no law. (Galatians 5:22-23)

But the fruit of the Spirit is love, joy, peace, patience, kindness, goodness, faithfulness, gentleness, self-control; against such things there is no law. *Galatians 5:22-23*

Speak To Him In Your Heart

Be still. Close your eyes. Feel His nearness. He is closer to you than your hands and feet are close to you. You are the temple of His Spirit. Thank Him for being there for you all these years even when you were not conscious of His nearness. Thank Him for His love for you even when your heart was cold toward Him. Thank Him for the gaze of His eyes on you even when you were not looking. Thank Him for hearing the cries of your heart even when you try to keep them to yourself and He was there waiting for you to put your head on His shoulder because He loves you. Take your time. Meditate on these images. Stay in His loving gaze. Speak to Him in humility and love.

So do not fear, for I am with you; do not be dismayed, for I am your God. I will strengthen you and help you; I will uphold you with my righteous right hand. (Isaiah 41:10)

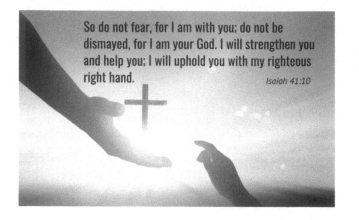

So do not fear, for I am with you; do not be dismayed, for I am your God. I will strengthen you and help you; I will uphold you with my righteous right hand.

Isaiah 41:10

Chapter Twenty-Seven

FAMILY OF GOD

"Believe in the Lord Jesus, and you will be saved, you and your household."
(Acts 16:31)

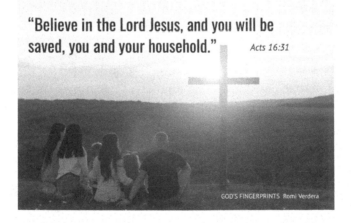

God Touched Me

My father's family were not church goers. As I was growing up,
I never saw my grandfather, aunts and uncles on my father's side go
to church or pray and have a relationship with God. My father on
the other hand, because he married my mother who was active in

our hometown church, became a God believer through the influence of my mother by the grace of God. He never joined any church organization and simply attends Sunday church service. But I saw my father learned to enjoy reading the Bible and became a prayerful man. I witnessed his transformation into being a follower of Jesus' teachings just by reading the Bible by himself every day, sitting down at his bed to pray simple prayers to God. He did not have any Christian instruction from anyone apart from going to church on Sunday, and reading and meditating on the word of God in the Bible. While a young boy, my father would talk to me about what Jesus said in the Gospel. He lived quietly and God took him at age 60 having lived a simple peaceful life.

My mother was active in the church. She was an organizer of people and activities in the church. She was very prayerful and tried to help people with what she had. She took care of the household chores when I and my three sisters were little kids while my father went to work. This faith in God was inherited by myself and my three sisters from our parents.

At age twenty-two, I married my wife Rosavilla who was also a God-loving woman. I believe my finding her is God's answer to the prayers of my parents that God may guide me in my life.

I have two adult sons who now have their own families too. They are married to God believing wives raising their children in the faith also. My wife always says she had been praying for both our boys to meet good wives. Now we pray that they are led and kept by the grace of God to continue in His ways.

———

My Heart's Response

Dear God, I thank you for the gift of family. I pray for those who are not so fortunate to have had one on this earth. I pray that they may know your love. You are our loving Father. I pray for everyone whose heart hungers for love that they may know You and experience Your love. May their hardened heart be softened by your touch. May their wounds be healed by your love. May they accept Jesus your Son as their brother. May they be filled by your Holy Spirit so that they may see the reality of the joy of being united to the whole human family reconciled by Jesus to you Father. Amen.

While Jesus was still talking to the crowd, his mother and brothers stood outside, wanting to speak to him. Someone told him, "Your mother and brothers are standing outside, wanting to speak to you."

He replied to him, "Who is my mother, and who are my brothers?" Pointing to his disciples, he said, "Here are my mother and my brothers. For whoever does the will of my Father in heaven is my brother and sister and mother. (Matthew 12:46-50)

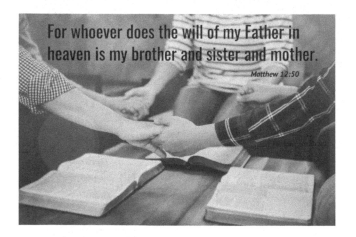

For whoever does the will of my Father in heaven is my brother and sister and mother.
Matthew 12:50

God Is Touching You

God wants to heal the wounds in your heart caused by family. God designed the family as a nurturing environment for His children. Unfortunately, just like anything God had designed, the human free will acting independently of God's will has done damages to God's design of family. One way or another, we all have good memories and bad memories of our family. Some have more of good, and others have more of bad memories that have left scars in the mind, heart and spirit. Allow God to touch your mind, heart, and soul. Allow God to heal you.

He heals the brokenhearted and binds up their wounds. (Psalm 147:3)

———

Speak To God In Your Heart

Be still. Imagine God looking at you with love. Give to Him all your anxieties and apprehensions. He knows what hinders you from feeling His love. Your mind knows that He loves you but your heart does not feel it because of past wounds. Give to Him your bad memories. They no longer exist except in your memory. The only reality is now, today. Today God is gazing at you with love. Let His love envelop you as the sunlight warms your skin. Let His love fill your soul as the air you breathe fills your lungs. Surrender to Him all your fears including the fear of not being accepted and loved. It is just a fear. It is not real. The reality is that God loves you. God sent His Son Jesus to tell us of the Father's love. Stay at this thought. Meditate on His love in Jesus. Take your time. Be still. Stay as long as necessary for this to be real in your consciousness. Thank Him for His love. Say it with your lips. Express to Him your love. You might not feel you love Him yet, but you know you want to love Him. You desire that you have more love of Him. That is good enough for God. He will pour His love into you. He will pour His Holy Spirit into your spirit.

For this reason I kneel before the Father, from whom every family in heaven and on earth derives its name. I pray that out of his glorious riches he may strengthen you with power through his Spirit in your inner being, so that Christ may dwell in your hearts through faith. And I pray that you, being rooted and established in love, may have power, together with all the Lord's holy people, to grasp how wide and long and high and deep is the love of Christ, and to know this love that surpasses knowledge—that you may be filled to the measure of all the fullness of God. (Ephesians 3:14-19)

I pray that out of his glorious riches he may strengthen you with power through his Spirit in your inner being, so that Christ may dwell in your hearts through faith.

Ephesians 3:16-17

Chapter Twenty-Eight

MY PEACE BE IN YOU

I remain confident of this, I will see the goodness of the LORD in the land of the living. (Psalm 27:13)

I remain confident of this, I will see the goodness of the LORD in the land of the living.

Psalm 27:13

God Touched Me

My life was not always sunshine and roses. I had a season in my life in my 30s when I wanted to kill myself because life was so dark and there were times when I cannot see the light at the end of the tunnel. But God never failed to show me some light to guide me out of those very dark moments that seemed hopeless at that time. I can still remember clearly a moment when I asked Jesus, "Lord, you said in Your words that You will give Your peace that the world cannot give. I need that peace now. I am so disturbed and in miserable pain deep inside of me." I knew I deserved my misery because of the wrongs things I have done, so I was asking God for mercy. I prayed it when I was so depressed and confused and almost suicidal. I was praying it on the way to the office where I used to work. I just could not shake off this deep depression inside of me. My mind was intellectually all tangled up with confusion about my self-created trouble, and my heart was experiencing a very deep sadness that would not go away. A few minutes after I prayed it, I arrived at the office and I can still recall clearly that moment I was standing by my desk when I was hit with this overwhelming "peace" that Jesus says He gives. All of a sudden, my depression lifted up and I was even awed by the experience because nothing had changed in the circumstances of my life and yet I had no negative thoughts, nor sad emotion any longer. It lasted for a while. That experience gave me a strong assurance that God is real, and He hears our prayers, and it is just a matter of time, I did not know how long then, that all will be well with me. I know that I will see His favor and goodness and He will restore my broken life.

Peace I leave with you; my peace I give you. I do not give to you as the world gives. Do not let your hearts be troubled and do not be afraid. (John 14:27)

Peace I leave with you; my peace I give you. I do not give to you as the world gives. Do not let your hearts be troubled and do not be afraid.
John 14:27

I had faith then that I would see God's restoration of my life on this earth and not just in the afterlife with Him in eternity. Life crises on this earth are meant to be overcome with God's help. Now I can look back and testify of God's forgiveness, mercy, love and restoration.

***

My Heart's Response

Dear God, I thank you for the peace, joy and love You pour into my heart. You are true to your promises. You say that heaven and earth will pass away but Your words will never pass away. You speak and the universe is created. You speak to my soul and peace is created within it. You say that Your words are like rain from heaven and when it falls on earth, it does not return back to You without having done the purpose for which You send it. I pray Father that You let Your fresh rain fall all over my life that I may have an abundance of life according to your design. I love You God. Amen.

So is my word that goes out from my mouth: It will not return to me empty, but will accomplish what I desire and achieve the purpose for which I sent it. (Isaiah 55:11)

———

God is Touching You

Whatever it is causing disturbances in your life, God wants to uproot it so that you may have peace. There is nothing too complicated for Him to arrange, nothing so broken that He cannot fix. That is what Jesus came here for; to free you from the prison of the limitation of your mind. You will experience that there is freedom in Christ and the knowledge of his love. Your mind is a prisoner of its thoughts and fears, and unless the mind is transformed into the mind of Jesus Christ, there is no peace and freedom. The mind is burdened by thoughts of unworthiness, self-doubt, identity crisis, and meaningless existence. Jesus came to heal the broken-hearted and set prisoners free. Meditate on the freedom in the spirit that Jesus offers.

For God has not given us a spirit of fear, but of power and of love and of a sound mind. (2 Timothy 1:7)

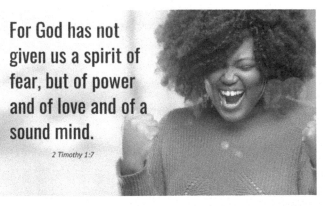

———

Speak To God In Your Heart

Be still. Meditate. Keep your mind quiet by focusing on your breathing. Feel the air coming in and out of your nostrils and lungs.

Relax. The whole universe is silent. Nature has a beautiful rhythm. Every atom in the universe is dancing to the tune of God's word. If there is any agitation inside of you, it is coming from your entanglement with the business affair of the people on this earth whom you are trying to please, or your attachment with them, or the lack of proper relationship with them. Or it may be caused by your need to survive, the needs of the body like food, shelter, clothing, housing, bank account, and others. Realize that God is the source of all harmony in our lives. If you are experiencing any disharmony within yourself, it is because you are not aligned to the peace of God. Speak to Jesus and ask for the peace that He promises He will give. Remind Him of His promise. He is just waiting for you to ask. Be still, dispose of yourself to receive this peace that only He can give. The world cannot give you this peace. Only Jesus can. Thank Him for it. Stay on the meditation of these words.

> *Peace I leave with you; my peace I give you. I do not give to you as the world gives. Do not let your hearts be troubled and do not be afraid. (John 14:27)*

———

Chapter Twenty-Nine

GOD IS NOT HIDING

My sheep hear my voice, and I know them, and they follow me. (John 10:27)

God Touched Me.

"I am actually not hiding. I speak every second. I am the good thoughts that pop up in your head all day long. You just do not realize it. People just do not hear Me, or do not recognize Me. I am your good conscience that nudges you to do the right thing. So, I send other people to you to speak My will in an audible voice. Most often they do not know they are speaking on My behalf, and most often you do not know that it is I who is speaking and talking to you."

For God speaks in one way, and in two, though man does not perceive it. (Job 33:14)

―――――

My Heart's Response

Dear God, how many times I have missed Your communication with me because I was so distracted. How many good ideas You have planted in my mind and I did not pay attention because I thought they were just my imagination. It is true, they were my imagination. What other tools would you communicate with me other than my own mind and my imagination? I thank You for these revelations of Your mind on my life Lord. I love You God. Amen.

I will listen to what God the Lord says; he promises peace to his people, his faithful servants. (Psalm 85:8)

―――――

God is Touching You

Some say that God does not speak anymore because He already spoke thousands of years ago through His prophets who wrote what He wanted to say. And all we have to do is read his words. I think most people mistake God's speaking as an audible voice that one should hear from God. God is interested in every little thing in your daily living. In general, God has spoken a guideline in His words in the Bible wherein He permits us to make choices in our lives. And for as long as those choices are not in violation of His will regarding our course of action, we can expect Him to help us in our chosen direction. But still, God says that His thoughts are far above our thoughts which means that in many instances where we have to choose between several good choices, God always knows the bes,t and we would want Him to show us which is the best one. So we need to hear from God today to make the best choices in the affairs of our lives.

For my thoughts are not your thoughts, neither are your ways my ways," declares the Lord. "As the heavens are higher than the earth, so are my ways higher than your ways and my thoughts than your thoughts. (Psalm 55:8-9)

———

Speak to God in Your Heart

Be still. Silence your mind and be aware that you are in God's presence. You can bring to Him all your concerns, questions, requests, supplications and petitions. He knows them all already but in bringing them up to Him, you are disposing yourself to His leadings as to what decisions to make and actions to take. Wait for His response. Be still. You might have to wait, and wait, and wait. That is alright. You should also speak to Him about those things before you sleep. Later on, by practicing this, you will experience that God answers even in your sleep. You might be awakened early in the morning, or you might have the answer as soon as you wake up as clear as day. There will be times you can see the answer so clearly and you know for sure it was from Him.

Therefore everyone who hears these words of mine and puts them into practice is like a wise man who built his house on the rock. (Matthew 7:24)

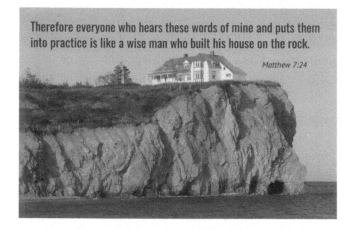

Chapter Thirty

A MAN HARVESTED

"Come, all you who are thirsty, come to the waters; and you who have no money, come, buy and eat!Come, buy wine and milk without money and without cost." (Isaiah 55:1-2)

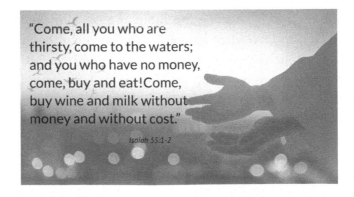

"Come, all you who are thirsty, come to the waters; and you who have no money, come, buy and eat!Come, buy wine and milk without money and without cost."

Isaiah 55:1-2

God Touched Me

My son and I were having breakfast one morning at our vacation house in the Philippines when I saw Alex from our big sliding glass door overlooking the front yard walked into the gate. Alex is the man whom we hire to drive our family around in the Philippines when we are on vacation there. He came in rushing at the gate at the front yard with a serious look on his face. I told my son to continue his breakfast while I came out to meet him. There was an outdoor metal round table with three chairs and we sat there to talk. He said he came because he had a lot of questions. Something happened the day before while he was driving my family around to visit one of my longtime friends, Jimmy. We picked Jimmy up and he led us to a nearby mall where we had dinner. While having dinner, I was talking to Jimmy across the table and Alex was sitting right next to him. My wife and my son's family were with us enjoying the dinner.

Somewhere in my conversation with my friend Jimmy, I mentioned that we can hear God when we read the Bible. There was nothing intense about my conversation with Jimmy. It was a casual light conversation. What I did not know was my statement "You can hear God when you read the Bible," hit the heart of Alex and planted a desire on him to hear too from God. After dinner we brought back Jimmy to his residence and Alex dropped us home.

That next morning, Alex told me what happened to him. He never read the Bible before. When he heard me say that a person can hear from God by reading the Bible, it gave him the desire to hear from God too. So when he got home that night, he looked for a Bible in their house and opened it. He brought that Bible with him to me that early morning. He wanted to hear from God the night before so he opened the Bible randomly to a page and it was Isaiah 55 where God is inviting him to come to Him because he is thirsty. And he kept on reading.

"Come, all you who are thirsty, come to the waters; and you who have no money, come, buy and eat!Come, buy wine and milk without money and without cost." (Isaiah 55:1-2)

One day while driving me around later, he said that he thought his life would just be driving people around and there is nothing more in his life. Today he is happy and finding God opened up a whole new world for him. He now goes to church regularly, became a part of a prayer group community, enjoys being part of the men's singing group. He reads the Bible now, prays to God, and finds a whole new meaning to his life.

––––––

My Heart's Response

Dear God, I find it such a wonderful privilege that You use my mouth to speak to another person. The thought of it gives me so much delight inside of me for knowing that You care enough to consider using me to be part of Your work in drawing people close to You.

For the Lord gives wisdom; from his mouth come knowledge and understanding. (Proverbs 2:6)

––––––

God Is Touching You

Be still. God wants you to know that you are a part of His grand design on this earth. That might seem mind-boggling to you but this whole universe and God's divine drama of creation is not complete without you. The design of the seashore is not complete if one grain of sand is missing. The whole heavenly body is not complete if one star is not there. He has the exact count of every star in the sky.

He determines the number of the stars and calls them each by name. (Psalm 147:4)

Do not for one moment think that you are insignificant. Meditate on this. Keep still. Let that truth sink into your consciousness until your heart feels the reality of your oneness with God who created every little DNA in your body. The same elements in the stars are in your body.

If you allow Him, He will use your mouth to bring comfort to others by putting His words in your mouth.

For it is not you who speak, but the Spirit of your Father speaking through you. (Matthew 10:20 ESV)

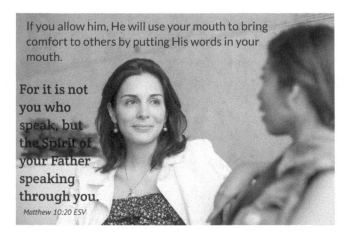

Speak To God In Your Heart

Be still. Put yourself in the presence of God. Leave all your cares behind. He knows all your cares. Ask Him to let you be aware of your place in His creation. You might not understand yet the clear picture of that reality. The important thing is you know now that you are a significant part of His design. In time, you will have more revelation of the truth of the reason for your existence. You will continue to search. God will continue to reveal. You might wonder why would He not just reveal everything to you at once. That is because He wants to build your relationship with Him as you seek answers from Him.

Now we see but a dim reflection as in a mirror; then we shall see face to face. Now I know in part; then I shall know fully, even as I am fully known. (1 Corinthians 13:12)

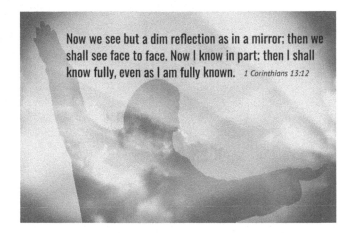

Now we see but a dim reflection as in a mirror; then we shall see face to face. Now I know in part; then I shall know fully, even as I am fully known.   *1 Corinthians 13:12*

Chapter Thirty-One

FRIEND IN LIFE

"I have called you friends, for everything that I learned from my Father I have made known to you." (John 15:15)

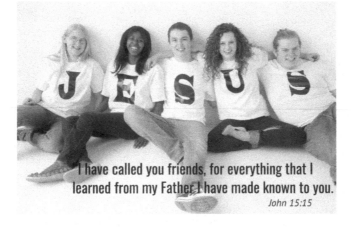

I have called you friends, for everything that I
learned from my Father I have made known to you.'
John 15:15

GOD TOUCHED ME

My wife and I were with a group of relatives and friends for the weekend at a Virginia farm. We stayed in a five-hundred year-old mansion with dark wood rooms surrounded by small private cabins you could rent as your lodging for the night. In the morning, we gathered together for breakfast in a dining room on the main building. Before I left my cabin to go to the dining room for breakfast, I was looking for my car keys all over the cabin because I did not find them in the pocket of my pants. I pride myself in not losing keys because I do not put them anywhere except in the pocket of my pants, or on a certain drawer at home, or in the pocket of my hand-carry bag. I do not like looking for things so I make sure I have limited places where I put them all the time, so I know where to look for them, especially my keys and my cell-phone. When I could not find it that morning, I started to think of worse scenarios. Maybe I left my keys inside the car which locks on its own when I step away, in which case I would have to call a locksmith to open my car, and we are half an hour away from the nearest civilization. Maybe I dropped it on the trail from my car in the parking lot to my cabin, which was kind of a long walk on a little dirt trail the previous night. But I looked and did not find it there. Maybe it accidentally dropped out of my pocket to the bed, or the couch, or the bathroom, but they were nowhere there. As we sat for breakfast, my wife ordered my food for me. I was disturbed thinking of worse scenarios I had to do if I do not find my keys, because I checked my car and it is locked. That means if they are inside the car, I would not be able to open it except with a locksmith. It was a Sunday morning at a farm half an hour away from the nearest local civilization. I stood up from my chair at the breakfast table and told everyone I will go back to our cabin while everyone is waiting for their food anyway. I will try to look for my keys again. On the way to my cabin, I whispered: "God, you know where my missing keys are right? And I am your friend because you told me so." That is another story by itself, how God woke me up two mornings in a row telling me that I am His friend. I continued, "God, friends help friends. I am your friend so help me find my keys. Show me where they are." As soon as I entered the cabin, I went straight to the closet to a jacket lying on some leaning object by the wall of the closet. I thought I left that jacket in my car the previous afternoon because it was kind of warm for a jacket that previous day. I searched its pockets and I found my keys. I went right back to the breakfast table and told everybody, "I found my keys. I asked my friend to help me find it." They looked at me like asking in their mind, "you have a friend here?" My nephew laugh and said, "that's God, his friend." I smiled. Yes, God is my friend and this kind of thing happened every now and then when I would ask Him to the rescue and He does come.

————

My Heart's Response

Dear God. Thank you for always being there for me. Sometimes I wonder why you let me stump my toes on the ground and I get hurt. Or You let me lose things and forget where I put them but then you show me after I call on You. Many times I struggle first on my own effort trying to solve my challenges by myself, and then later realize I did not ask You for help right away, so I just prolonged my agony. I should have asked right away to shorten my distress. But then my memory of Your goodness is so short, I keep forgetting. I am part of humanity that barely learns from history, and we forget easily the good things You have done for us over and over again. Forgive us Lord.

————

God Is Touching You

Think of the time you needed help, and there was nobody to help you. Imagine yourself in your distressing situation, and you did not even think of God, or you thought of God and you think He does not care about solving this little or big problem that you were having. You think that He has other things on His mind to pay attention to. Yours was just a common problem that common people simply try to solve on their own without God's help because it is not too important to God. Or maybe you think your situation is so great for God to solve. Imagine Him lovingly watching you struggle waiting for you to ask Him for help. You might say, why does He not just do it and help you without you asking Him? That is because for God, the development of your relationship with Him is more important than any solution to your struggle. If He does that all the time without you asking, you would not even know that He is there, and you would not care about knowing Him. He wants to be intimate with you. By answering your cry for help, He is able to build intimacy with you.

"... You do not have because you do not ask God." James 4:2

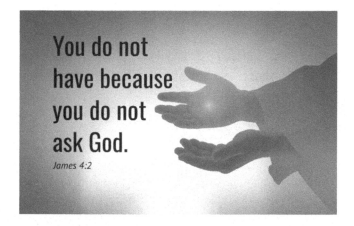

Keep your mind for a longer time imagining that He was there watching you lovingly on your struggle, willing to help but waiting for your call for help. Then imagine Him with you right now watching you as you ponder Him.

Speak To God In Your Heart

Be still. Put yourself in the presence of God. He wants to be your friend. Ponder that. Why would He want to be your friend? Try to understand that the only reason He created you is to share His life with you because He loves you. It His nature to love. He cannot be anything else but love. He cannot be indifferent. That is not in His nature. God is ever-expanding His life through you. Thank Him for giving you existence and for the fact that you are an extension of His life. If you allow Him, He will use you to bring life to others too through you. He is your friend. You are not only His child but also His friend. Some children are not friends of their human fathers. God wants to be your intimate friend. Speak to Him. Let Him know you too want to be His friend. Meditate on this.

"Abraham believed God, and it was credited to him as righteousness," and he was called God's friend. (James 2:23)

"Abraham believed God, and it was credited to him as righteousness," and he was called God's friend.
James 2:23

ABOUT THE BOOK

This book will help you to experience the touch of God. When you allow His touch, you allow miracles to happen to your life.

"For I know the plans I have for you," declares the Lord, "plans to prosper you and not to harm you, plans to give you hope and a future. (Jeremiah 29:11 NIV)

Later, you will look back and see God's fingerprints all over your life and you will have become the best version of yourself, a person after God's own heart.

In this book you will learn:

- How to enjoy being in God's presence.
- How to receive your miracles.
- How to be at peace and not worry.
- How to quiet your mind and listen to God.
- How to grow spiritually through meditation.

ABOUT THE AUTHOR

ROMI VERDERA

Successful global entrepreneur, Christian lay teacher, studied in a
seminary for 8 years, taught theology at a university, inspirational
speaker, philanthropist, father, husband, grandpa, world traveler,
writer. Romi shares on how he experienced spiritual living of peace,
joy, love and financial prosperity.

https://romiverdera.tv

 facebook.com/romi.verdera